The Perfect Shot for Dinosaurs

BY
PHIL MASSARO

WITH ARTWORK BY
LAURIE O'KEEFE

SAFARI PRESS

T0163176

Dedicated to my mother, Paula,
for inspiring me and giving me the courage
to embrace a lifetime of adventures.

Massaro, Phil

O'Keefe, Laurie (artist)

First edition

Safari Press

2019, Long Beach, California

ISBN 978-1-57157-504-3

Library of Congress Catalog Card Number: 2018943240

10 9 8 7 6 5 4 3 2 1

Printed in Korea

Readers wishing to see Safari Press's many fine books on big-game hunting, wingshooting, and sporting firearms should visit our website at safaripress.com.

CONTENTS

FOREWORD

I am, or maybe it's better to say "was" a highly regarded paleontologist specializing in carnivorous theropods. In laymen's terms, that makes me a scientist with a special concentration on Hollywood's favorite three-toe, meat-eating dinosaurs. Up until a few short years ago I spent my days mulling over the ancient remains of Tyrannosaurus, Allosaurus, Velociraptor, and Spinosaurus, amongst others. I came to prominence for my ground-breaking lab work on prehistoric metabolic function, but I achieved my real renown as a field expert by going on countless global expeditions to hunt live dinosaurs, journeys that took me from the Liaoning province to Beijing to the Badlands of Utah . . . and back.

As a scientist, skepticism is at the forefront of my trade, and absolute proof in the scientific community is hard to come by. Some of the most well-known scientific evidence such as the existence of gravity is still regarded as "theory." Theories are always shrouded with doubt until the scientific method is thoroughly exercised, tested, and retested by so many scientists that the results become obvious. Even then, in the face of overwhelming data, these ideas may still be only theory.

What I am about to present, as outlandish as it may sound, is, indeed, fact and not theory. What I'm about to share with you should be met with absolute skepticism, but skepticism alone in never enough for complete dismissal. This information cost me both my career and my reputation. So, before you add your name to the legions of others who have derisively mocked my work, think long and hard about my motives and the price I've paid. After all, I've voyaged from, literally, the top of my field to descend to the low strata of a misanthropic recluse. I assure you it was for good reason. Now, open your mind to the possibilities and consider this: Dinosaurs never went extinct and they roam the Earth to this very day.

As best as I can currently understand, those species of dinosaurs that have survived have evolved the ability to hibernate underground. With the use of their hybrid metabolic cycles, they bury themselves underground, sometimes for periods of centuries at a time. Much like a wood frog, their hearts will actually cease to beat, and ice crystals form in their blood. They enter this state of torpor that more closely resembles an autonomous cryogenic freezing. I haven't figured out exactly how or why they do this, but when they emerge they are utterly ravenous.

"Ravenous" is not a word I use lightly. The herbivores awake to decimate huge tracts of forest and fields of vegetation. I speculate that some of the asymmetrical crop-circles popularized on far-flung television programs are actually the methodic consumption of plant life by dinosaurs.

On the other hand, the carnivores are so inherently destructive and murderous that it is no wonder there have been so few credible eyewitnesses.

These beasts have outlived their welcome on our planet. They represent a very real threat to both our fragile ecosystem and humanity at large. I'm sure if we spared no expense, we could capture some and keep them in a zoo, or perhaps set them on a large deserted island where we could study them, much like was done in the famous movie *Jurassic Park*. We all know how well that worked. The rest, however, need to be eliminated.

Enter the author of this book, Philip P. Massaro. Phil is an experienced hunter, ballistics expert, author, and television host. He has hunted and felled big-game species on many continents. He has designed and implemented specialized ammunition for a multitude of hunting scenarios. He is a well-regarded and sought-after expert in each of his fields. Phil has read all of my work with none of the disdain of my former colleagues. He digested my discourse on prehistoric metabolic states as well as my journal entries on dinosaur anatomy and nerve function.

After multiple email exchanges with my seemingly one true advocate, we decided to meet up at a local gastropub called The Cask and Rasher. Over a few stouts and more than a few bourbons, we came to realize that we are distant cousins whose great-great grandfathers were brothers. Upon this revelation, I shot up from my seat to grab a well-worn book clad in reptile leather. It had been my great-great grandfather's journal. I had often regarded the exploits therein on dragon hunting to be purely satirical. Could it be that our ancestors hunted these terrible lizards over a hundred years ago?

Fate be tempted, we sold off our assets and plotted a course to Zambia, the location of the last recorded journal entry. From there we began our pursuit.

What you hold in your hands is the result of our years-long safari after the great dinosaurs of yesteryear, a quintessential guide to the weapons, cartridges, and techniques for hunting the most dangerous big game the Earth has ever known. May it take you on the fantastic journeys that Phil and I have shared.

Welcome, fellow believers, to *The Perfect Shot for Dinosaurs*.

Jarrett M. Lane
Coxsackie, New York
March 15, 2018

Phil Massaro's (left) and Jarrett Lane's great-gre grandfathers out for the day hunting dinosaur circa 1880.

INTRODUCTION

I have been among the great beasts of the earth—lion, elephant, buffalo on several continents, bears. None of them compare to hunting the greatest of game: the dinosaur. The very name is Greek for "terrible lizard," but even that loose translation doesn't do them justice. Seven trips to the Dark Continent, being lost in the Australian Outback, and numerous trips to the wilds of North America in pursuit of the largest mammals all pale in comparison to my great passion: the hunt for dinosaurs. They command attention at all points, and they bring a level of excitement that make a Cape buffalo at ten paces seem like a committee meeting, they make the fury of a charging elephant seem like Girl Scouts selling cookies at the door.

Should you be one of the few who have been in the presence of Tyrannosaurus rex, that King of predators, you understand. If you've not had that experience, no words I may put in print can describe the meeting, but within the confines of this volume I fully intend to prepare you to be as well-equipped as possible. The mental preparation is as important as the choice of firearm; your mind must be as solid as your rifle, and the tactics required will call upon your skills as a hunter as much as your skills as a shooter. This is no deer hunt; this is no ritualistic get-together of buddies to shoot the breeze as much as to shoot birds. This is a very serious affair that only the strongest-willed hunter should pursue, and only the strongest will survive.

The docile dinosaurs—those portrayed in movies and books as gentle giants—can end your life in a heartbeat. You must become an apex predator yourself, and you must call upon all the instincts

Phil Massaro and his favorite Heym Express rifle, in Tyrannosaur camp.

My great-grandfather Filippo Massaro (right) and his brother Jack, examining dinosaur bones in Utah circa 1880.

programmed into your DNA to survival. A dinosaur can show up at the most inopportune time, so prepare your mental self and carry the firearm that will see that you are not immediately written into the history books.

My first encounter came when I was a much younger man, long before my hair fell out and the gray appeared in my beard. I am a licensed land surveyor by trade, and during my apprenticeship under my father—dear old Grumpy Pants—we were out in the remote woods of my native Greene County, New York, locating a stream that just happened to be the boundary between properties.

While meandering downstream through the hemlock forest, I saw something I'd never seen before, and immediately called my father away from the transit to show him what I'd found: large, three-toe, clawed tracks that were bigger than my footprint. They were also fresh in the moist soil on the western edge of the stream. Grumpy Pants uttered one word, "Velociraptor." That, of course, ended our work for that day.

We backtracked, for we were unarmed with the exception of surveying tools and a machete for clearing the line of sight. Proceeding to the nearest convenience store for a cup of coffee, we stood in silence, consumed with our recent experience. To this day, we work with nothing less than a powerful handgun on hip; we are now noticeably wary.

My childhood fascination with those creatures that science has wrongly deemed as extinct, coupled with a hunter's education in my youth, has prepared me for a life of adventure, calling upon all my skills, in pursuit of these Terrible Lizards. I have been silent about my hunts for dinosaurs until now, but my silence has been broken with the publishing of this tome. Should you find yourself in the wild places, as I have, stumbling upon the track of a creature that has the power to destroy anything in its path, I want you prepared, lest you suffer the sleepless nights and recurring nightmares that have been my constant companions these many years.

Welcome to *The Perfect Shot for Dinosaurs*.

SOME NOTES ON GUNS AND LOADS

Throughout this book you will find references to both common and obscure calibers, not to mention some rifles that are usually reserved for pursuit of the largest mammals on the planet, namely the African Big Five. These five great beasts are the closest animals in size that can be correlated to the wide variety of Terrible Lizards of the dinosaur world.

The .470 Nitro Express makes a great choice for double rifles. Ammo is plentiful, and the cartridge is very effective.

DINOSAUR CARTRIDGES

Historically, I'd feel comfortable saying that at the turn of the twentieth century mankind had finally developed a formula that would cleanly take any and all of the world's great game animals. That's when the .450 Nitro Express, loaded with 480-grain cupro-nickel solid bullets, first came on the hunting scene. John Rigby & Company, the prestigious firm that had its roots in Dublin, Ireland, and later in London, England, developed the cartridge, and for well over a century it has remained the benchmark by which dangerous-game cartridges are measured.

Many of the common double-rifle cartridges, like the .470 NE, the .475 No. 2 Jeffery, the .500/465, and many others were designed to replicate the ballistic formula of the .450, using a 480- or 500-grain bullet and having a muzzle velocity of 2,150 fps. The .458 Winchester Magnum was also designed with this formula in mind, and it filled the need in a bolt-action rifle. Jack Lott's modern update, the .458 Lott, bettered the design. The formula works, and it's a great choice for the dinosaur hunter.

However, modern bullet technology has taken some of the classic African "medium"-bore cartridges—and here I'm referring to the .375 Holland & Holland Belted Magnum, .404 Jeffery, .416 Rigby, and .416 Remington Magnum—into a class heretofore unavailable. Where once the 480- and 500-grain bullets of the .450s were considered the penultimate design for both energy and penetration, modern bullet designs for these lighter cartridges have shown unparalleled field performance on the largest game animals.

The traditional qualities of these cartridges—and all were renowned for their penetration—have been improved through the designs of the projectiles they use. For example, Norma's African PH line of ammunition is built around heavy-for-caliber projectiles (350-grain bullets in the .375, and 450-grain bullets in the .416s and .404), giving wonderful

The Heym Express in .404 Jeffery is a good all-around choice for most dinosaur hunting.

sectional density figures. Yes, the muzzle velocities have been reduced—on average about 250 fps—but the penetration is unprecedented, and that's the exact quality you'll need when hunting dinosaurs.

The true heavyweight cartridges I mention throughout this book offer a huge leap in both kinetic energy and bullet weight yet require a shooter to manage the sometimes horrific recoil. The .500 Nitro Express, the .505 Gibbs Magnum, and the .500 Jeffery use bullets between 535 and 600 grains, and when it comes to the up-close-and-personal encounters, they all give an additional sense of security, but only if the shooter can handle the gun properly.

That statement is even more applicable when discussing the .577 and .600 Nitro Express and the bolt-action cartridges like the .577 Tyrannosaur and .585 Nyati. Recoil can be hellacious, and the rifle must be built like a tank to handle it properly.

If one reads classic Africana hunting literature, especially the writing of the famous Capt. Walter Dalrymple Maitland "Karamojo" Bell, you'll see that he felt penetration, not sheer horsepower, was key to quickly dispatching the huge

For a lightweight, portable double rifle, the Heym 89B in .450/400 3-inch Nitro Express makes a very sensible choice.

pachyderms. His experiences hunting elephants across Africa with a number of diversified cartridges might be comparable to our pursuit of the Terrible Lizards. So, how does a dinosaur hunter go about choosing a cartridge?

The answer lies in a combination of self-evaluation and common sense. There's absolutely no point in investing your money in a huge cartridge if you cannot shoot it effectively. I'll be the first to admit that the .577 Tyrannosaur is a better cartridge for hunting its namesake than is the .404 Jeffery, but I'll also point out that a .577 bullet that misses the animal's brain is worthless, and a .404 bullet in the brain will get the job done.

So, the first step in the process of determining what is the best choice for you is to check your ego at the door and to be honest with yourself regarding your recoil limit. Try the heavy cartridges, and if you can't comfortably put two or three quick shots (depending on the rifle configuration), drop down the scale until you can. I can use the .505 Gibbs, but I am much more effective with the .470 Nitro Express.

Yes, I'm aware that I'm giving up frontal diameter and about 100 grains of bullet weight, but my shots are better placed. I've

Anchor that huge predator with the Barnes Banded Solid. It is a design that may very well save your life.

used the .470 for a Tyrannosaur—loaded with 500-grain North Fork Cup Point Solids—and it worked, but next time I'll opt for a heavier cartridge. The shaking hands, dry mouth, and weak legs that followed the experience had little to do with wanting a heavier cartridge; it had everything to do with the sheer terror that a predator of these proportions can engender.

PROJECTILES FOR THE DINOSAUR HUNTER

There are a few instances where a softpoint is called for, especially for the lighter dinosaurs, yet I firmly believe that in all instances a premium softpoint should get the nod. I am a huge fan of the Swift A-Frame, as it has its front core bonded to the jacket, and the copper partition will prevent the bullet from coming apart. The Barnes TSX is another good choice, but make sure it is of sufficient weight. The monometal construction will certainly hold together, and the expansion will destroy blood-rich tissue.

The relatively-unknown Peregrine Bullet Co. from South Africa makes a pair of worthy softpoints for dinosaurs. The Bushmaster is a unique monometal flat point, with a hollow cavity capped with a bronze plunger. Upon impact, the plunger compresses the air cavity,

Modern bullets, like the North Fork Cup Point Solid, increase the effectiveness of some older cartridge designs.

driving the walls of the ogive out in a radial direction, guaranteeing expansion. The same principal is employed in their PlainsMaster bullet, but it is a spitzer boat-tail design, to be used for longer ranges. Do some research into premium softpoints before making your choice, and spare no expense.

It is the solid, nonexpanding bullets that will occupy your cartridge belt more often than not. Choose the strongest designs—there are many good ones—that will give straight-line penetration. Among the modern designs, I am a fan of the Trophy Bonded Sledgehammer as loaded by Federal, the Barnes Banded Solid, the Woodleigh FMJ, the North Fork Flat Point, the Hornady DGS, and the Nosler Solid Bullet. All give a stellar performance and will stand up to even the thickest hide and bones, ensuring that a properly placed shot will reach the vital organs. I generally prefer those constructed of a homogenous metal to those of steel-jacketed lead, but the latter design can and will also give good performance.

The modern "expanding solids"—though that term may be an oxymoron—give a bit more flexibility. I am a huge proponent of the Woodleigh Hydrostatically Stabilized Solid, with its engineered "cup" at the nose because it gives perfect straight-line penetration yet creates a cavitation bubble that bursts blood vessels in a ten- to twelve-inch cylinder along the path of the bullet. I firmly believe this is the bullet of the future and is my No. 1 go-to choice for any dinosaur, anywhere.

Swift A-Frame bullets recovered from dinosaurs of various sizes.

North Fork's Cup Point Solid comes in just behind it, giving the slightest amount of expansion at the nose, and yet will still give fantastic penetration.

RIFLES FOR THE DINOSAUR HUNTER

Choosing a rifle for dinosaur hunting can be complicated, and you may end up with more than one rifle, depending on how diversified your hunting will be. There are affordable choices, for those on a budget, and among them I count the Winchester Model 70 Safari Express, the CZ550 Safari Magnum, and the Sako 85 Safari. All are dependable, and all offer a great value, yet these are restricted to the cartridges that will function in a bolt-action rifle.

The Peregrine Bushmaster is one of the best modern softpoints for giving reliable expansion and penetration.

I shan't address the age-old argument of bolt actions vs. double-rifles herein, as both have their strong suits, but for a hunter on a budget, the rifles just mentioned will certainly get the job done. If your budget allows, look to the more refined bolt rifles, like the Rigby Big Game (the .416 and .450 Rigby are both solid choices) and the Heym Express by Martini (especially in .505 Gibbs). Both have excellent balance, are stocked properly for fast, effective shooting, and are designed for a lifetime of good service.

Among the double rifles, the inexpensive models are a poor choice. I'm not one to say that a six-figure sum needs to be spent, but do not cheap-out when it comes to a double. Yes, you have two shots, but only two shots, and the rifle must be of utmost quality. I find that the designs with two-triggers and ejectors will give a decided advantage when the excrement hits the oscillator; the single-trigger designs will leave you with a useless club should something go wrong with the trigger; and the nonejector models will require too much time to reload when seconds count.

If money isn't an issue, there is nothing wrong with the purchase of a Holland & Holland, Westley Richards, John Rigby & Company, William Evans, or Purdey double, though I will say they come with a hefty price tag, often in excess of $75,000. I find the Heym Model 89B, a recent offering in the double-rifle market, to be the consummate value among modern double rifles, giving the balance and feel of a classic English double rifle, yet taking full advantage of German precision and modern steel.

My own rifle is an 89B, chambered in .470 Nitro Express, and I feel very confident carrying it into the most dangerous of situations. No matter what you choose, make sure the rifle is proven at the rifle range and that you do an appropriate amount of practice shooting, loading and reloading the gun in a variety of hunting situations.

For those situations where a military crew is needed, be sure your entire team is familiar with the operation of the weapon.

This Heym Model 89B in .470 Nitro Express is the author's go-to double rifle.

An M60 machine gun if improperly headspaced will give fits and may cause the loss of your animal. Likewise, if the M2 machine gun is to be employed, everyone on the team needs to be able to assemble, disassemble, and fire Ma Deuce. Your efforts will invariably be rewarded by intense training.

OPTICS

I'll be brief here, and it should be common sense, but when it comes to a good binocular and riflescope: Buy the best glass you can afford. The nightmare that could ensue should your scope fail to hold its zero and your shot be placed errantly is something that no dinosaur hunter need experience. If you can't afford the proper gear, postpone your hunt until you can. Hard-kicking rifles will make a mockery of cheap glass and second-rate mounts. Quality glass is not expensive, it is costly, yet the value is beyond mere cost.

A rack of suitable dinosaur hunting rifles.

INTRODUCTION TO AQUATIC DINOSAURS

Mankind's history of seafaring details hundreds of tales of unknown terrors, and not all were proved unfounded. For millennia, man has taken to the vast waters of our planet, and the tales of horror that have been handed down are attributed, as often as not and with varying degrees of accuracy, to those dinosaurs that still cruise the oceans. For sailors getting ready to set sail, these tales fill them with a sense of dread.

Few waterways are safe from those predatory monsters of a bygone era, save the minor streams and tributaries, and even those are questionable. America was founded by people who had little aversion to the sea, and I firmly believe with that comes a genetic predisposition to dealing with the oceans and all that comes with it. Surviving a trip on the oceans and dealing with those trials and tribulations associated with it, is one thing. Pursuing those beasts that have inspired the multitude of nautical nightmares is an entirely different matter.

Not only will your seamanship be tested, but hunting the mega-fauna of the oceans may very well be the culmination of all of your skills as a hunter and adventurer. The pursuit can bring you not only into international waters, but to the shores of many countries, hostile and friendly. Hone your linguistic skills and channel your inner Indiana Jones: The hunt for the aquatic dinosaurs will require a fair share of negotiation with authorities, and you'd better be prepared to accept the hardships that will come with an extended time at sea.

Be prepared to experience failure; the rewards are few and far between when hunting the aquatic dinosaurs. Nonetheless, do not falter, for the glory once you've bagged a Mosasaur or Plesiosaur is virtually unparalleled. And, if you ever thought that deer hunters were jealous over territory, you ain't seen nothin' yet when it comes to rivalry among dinosaur hunters! Novice hunters of aquatic dinosaurs will do their best to find out what waters you're hunting. Tactics of evasion are an absolute necessity, and you'll want to make sure your notes and charts are under lock and key at all times.

Bon voyage!

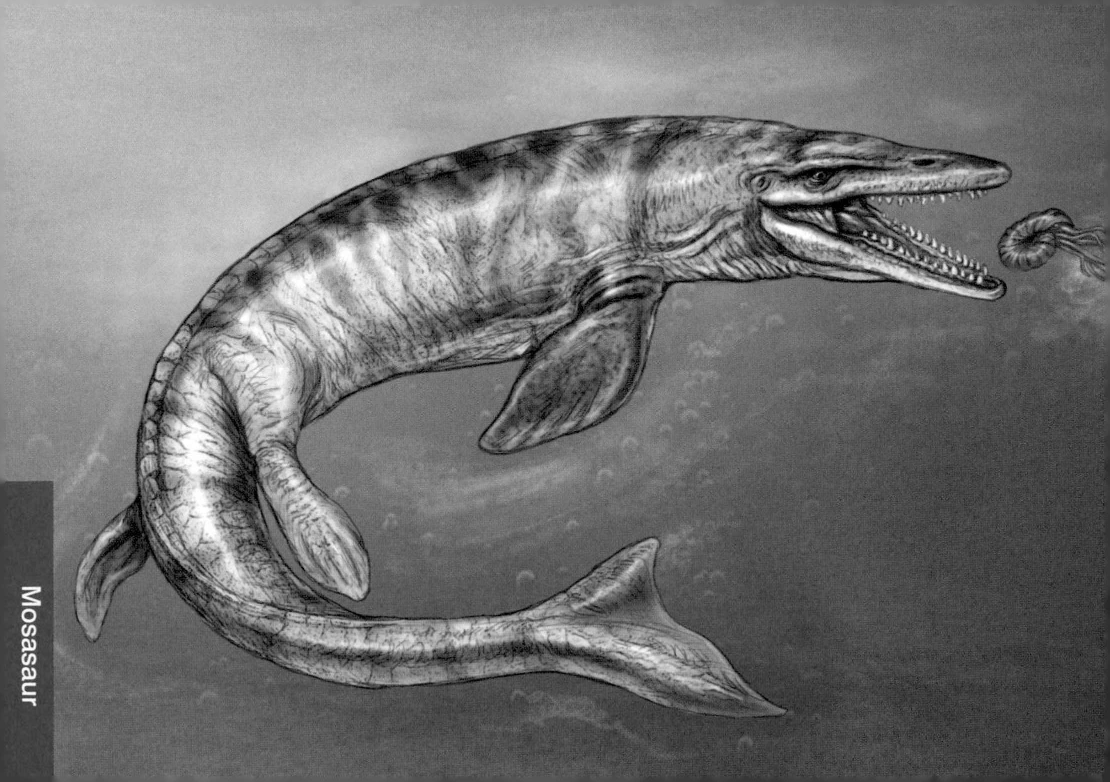

Mosasaur

MOSASAUR—THE DEMON OF THE WATER
CHAPTER 1

If you believe in the true terrors of the ocean–and there are many–a beach takes on an entirely new meaning to you, for it can become the gateway to the world of nightmares. Krakens, sharks, rogue whales, sea serpents, Homer's Scylla, even Cthulhu himself are all the stuff of seafaring nightmares, but they pale in comparison to the most efficient marine predator ever to grace the waters of planet Earth: the Mosasaur.

This sleek, scaled, air-breathing predator prefers warmer, shallower bodies of water, where it awaits, silently, ready to ambush its prey. In spite of its size, it is fast, equipped with four powerful fins and a strong tail, but that is nothing compared to its terrible mouth. Two rows of razor-sharp teeth spread in a V-pattern from the terminus of the jaw and complemented by a palate full of secondary teeth allow a Mosasaur to clamp onto its prey like the strongest forged-steel trap. The fate of a prey animal is predetermined; once you're in the five-foot-long jaws of a Mosasaur, prepare to meet your Maker.

I was sitting comfortably in a wooden beach chair, with one of those faux palm umbrellas overhead, no more than forty feet from the line where the bright blue waters of the Caribbean meets the white sand of Punta Cana, Dominican Republic. As we relaxed and watched the beautiful ocean, a pretty, young senorita brought my wife and me our second round of margaritas.

Lulled to somnolence by the peaceful aquatic scene of porpoises leaping gaily in the foam maybe three hundred yards or so out, I was suddenly jerked to the present, nearly choking on my margarita in the

Mosasaur

process. What was so alarming to have caused this reaction? As a young porpoise broke water, its entire body clearing the surface, a behemoth creature with a mouthful of daggers came up from the watery depth from behind it. The "Thing" opened its titanic mouth and neatly caught the porpoise whole before submerging into the depths again.

My eyes widened as I heard the young waitress say something urgent yet unintelligible in Spanish. All the native Dominicans hurriedly left the beach. I saw what I saw, and I know I saw it. I also knew immediately what it was: a large, trophy Mosasaur. I knew I would have one helluva time explaining to my wife why we wouldn't be swimming for the rest of our vacation.

WHERE TO FIND THEM

What's left of the remaining Mosasaur population can usually be found in warm, coastal waters, though there is a healthy herd in the Sargasso Sea, as well as in the northern Mediterranean. They have been taken as far north as the coast of Delaware, and as far south as Namibia's Skeleton Coast. They may be seen–rarely–off Baja California, and the waters off the north shore of Australia are a good place to hunt them. The warm Indian Ocean off Dar es Salaam, Tanzania, has been a source of sightings, for they've been feeding on the trade

The .50 BMG, shown next to a .30-'06 Springfield cartridge for scale.

The Perfect Shot for Dinosaurs

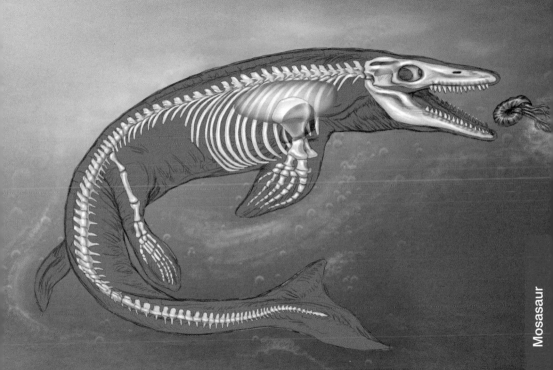

Mosasaur

ships that have been populating those waters for centuries. The best place to find a Mosasaur is anywhere in the coastal waters just mentioned, and you'd better be ready when you do confront one.

THE HUNT

A Mosasaur needs to surface in order to obtain oxygen, and that's how you'll spot them: breaching to breathe. The best method to get a shot at a Mosasaur is to find a dead whale or a very large fish with lots of sharks and other scavengers feeding on it. Drift your boat within two hundred yards of the feeding frenzy,

The famous M2, "Ma Deuce," fires a .50BMG cartridge. A belt-fed, crew-served weapon is the best choice for a Mosasaur.

and have the captain keep the boat aligned so that the shooter has a proper view of the bait. The feeding activity is certain to draw the attention of a Mosasaur, and you'll get your shot as it breaches after prey or to breathe.

Like an elephant hunt, this is a team effort. Who pulls the trigger matters not—a trophy Mosasaur belongs to everyone involved in the affair. You'll need to find a crew that knows how to keep its mouth shut; you do not want to reveal the best hunting spots for these highly desired trophies.

The Perfect Shot for Dinosaurs

Mosasaur

The sheer bulk of a Mosasaur will prevent the entire animal from being brought back to shore, even on the biggest and baddest fishing boat. Instead, gaff the head, secure it to the transom, and sever the head from the neck. When you bring that head on board through the tuna door, keep your hands and feet clear; the severed head of a Mosasaur will maintain enough muscle reflex for hours after death to cut a man in half. Take the teeth to a taxidermist you trust; he can make an attractive plaque out of them for your trophy room.

SHOT PLACEMENT

Your best bet for anchoring a Mosasaur is to deliver a shot to the brain, as little more than the head will usually breach water.

GUNS FOR THE MOSASAUR

A Mosasaur can weigh fifteen tons and measure up to fifty-feet long, so it's no easy feat to take down a Mosasaur. You'll have very little time for the shot, and you'll need some serious firepower. This is no place for an ordinary hunting rifle. Should you be able to procure a belt-fed, crew-served weapon such as

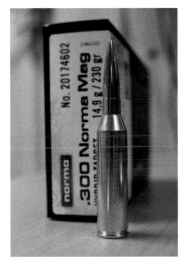

Adopted by the U.S. military for its long-range capabilities, the .300 Norma Magnum will definitely handle brain shots on a Mosasaur.

Mosasaur

The Perfect Shot for Dinosaurs

Mosasaur

The pin-point accuracy of the .338 Norma Magnum is a good choice for sniping a Mosasaur on the water.

the M60 machine gun, or even better the proven "Ma Deuce" .50 BMG machine gun, your boat will be well equipped for handling a Mosasaur.

If a machine gun is unavailable, you'll want a good sniper rifle of heavy caliber, capable of carrying its energy out to 400 and 500 yards. At a minimum, the .338 Lapua with 300-grain, full-metal-jacket bullets will get the job done, though the .408 CheyTac is a better choice. A Barrett rifle, in .50 BMG, is the best of the lot; just make sure you can get prone on the tuna tower of the boat, with a solid mat and rest. Keep a 12-gauge bang stick handy, and should you try to recover your Mosasaur, pay the insurance with a slug to the head, no matter how dead it appears.

The .338 Lapua is a wonderfully accurate and hard-hitting choice for head shots on a Mosasaur.

Mosasaur

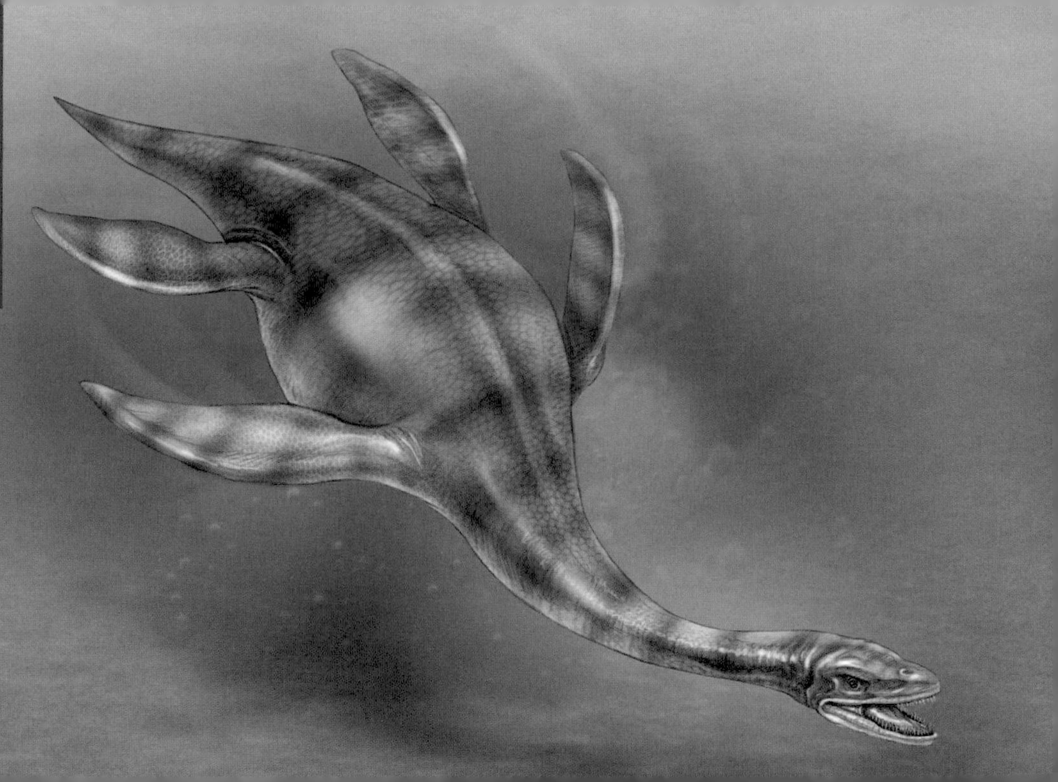

Plesiosaurus

PLESIOSAURUS—NESSIE OR NOT?
CHAPTER 2

I was in Scotland on a hunt for a red stag at a rather prestigious estate, thoroughly enjoying myself in the classic Highland setting. The post-hunt dram of fine Scotch—most welcome after coming "off-the-hill"—was being quaffed when talk among the hunters turned to the inhabitants of the multitude of lochs that dot the Scottish countryside. Being a stranger in a strange land, I was all ears, especially when the talk turned to the famous "Nessie," the resident Highland sea monster.

One dram led to another when a resident Scotsman had apparently heard enough of the routine theories and said, "Come owt-side with mee, Laddy, and I'll tell ya the trooth."

I couldn't resist the offer.

Now, I was born and raised in upstate New York, a couple hours south of the famous setting of the *Last of the Mohicans*, and I have spent my fair share of time in and around both Lake George and Lake Champlain, the latter being home to "Champ," our native counterpart to Nessie. So, I was immediately enthralled with the opportunity to discuss the facts of the case. The informant, a gentleman we'll call Simon, poured us each another dram before beginning to wag his tongue.

"You know, Laddy, Nessie is a Plesiosaur, right? I mean, you'd have to be a right numpty not to understand that, aye?"

I nodded in agreement, not letting on that I come from a place with its own—albeit less famous—water monster.

"I've seen *THEM*. That's right, there's more than just a single Nessie floatin' about in the lochs. At this point he lowered his voice and leaned closer. "I can tell you a see-cret, right? You seem trustworthy enough."

Again, like a child about to learn the origins and truths of Christmas, I nodded, feigning a bit of disinterest in the matter, though I was ready to burst.

"I've hunted one, Laddy. It's true, though the lot here wouldn't believe me if I showed it to them."

I couldn't resist the temptation and began to ask questions in the machine-gun fashion that only a toddler can possess.

"Well, the hunt is combination of fishing and proper shooting," Simon related, "and you've got to put out a suitable bait—I prefer rotted salmon—and sit nearby in yer boat with a stalking rifle."

Baiting! Ingenious! Why hadn't I thought of that?!?

Despite the idyllic setting—we were on the grounds of an ancient castle—my mind drifted to Lake Champlain and that silhouette I had seen two-plus decades ago. . . . It had to have been a Plesiosaurus.

******

The Plesiosaurus, a four-finned aquatic dinosaur with a long neck and shorter tail, preys upon smaller fish and sea life. Possessing a mouth full of sharp, conical teeth, a Plesiosaur will rise from the depths and use its powerful jaws to crush its prey, though it has been known to scavenge from time to time. Using the wide fins to propel itself through the water, the Plesiosaurus can and will remain submerged for long periods of time, though it has one definite personality flaw: It is a curious animal, and it's easily attracted to flashes and shiny objects.

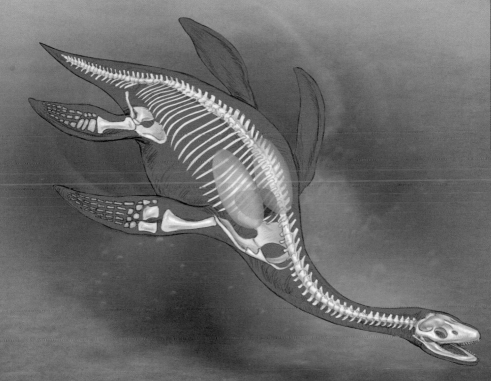

Weighing nearly one thousand pounds, and measuring in excess of ten feet from nose to tail tip, the Plesiosaurus is a formidable foe when encountered on the water. It can flip a small boat easily, resulting in drowned seamen and sunken craft.

THE HUNT

Baiting a Plesiosaurus is the smartest technique available. Any sort of fishing gear—including heavy duty shark hooks and braided line—are a waste of time. Use multiple large, shiny metal fishing spoons to draw the beast to the surface, but the shooter must be ready for action, for the head won't stay above water long, especially once the animal becomes aware he's being hunted.

SHOT PLACEMENT

A Plesiosaurus has a relatively shallow body—often not more than 3½ feet thick. You need to draw the Plesiosaurus to the surface where a head shot can dispatch it neatly. An accurate rifle with a scope of decent magnification will be required to place

The 6.5-284 Norma has the horsepower and precision required to get the job done, at ranges from "up-close-and-personal" to the next zip code.

The Perfect Shot for Dinosaurs

a precise shot in the brain, and I feel that practice from a boat is absolutely warranted.

GUNS AND HUNTING GEAR

Any accurate deer rifle from the 6.5mms up to the .30 calibers will suffice for the Plesiosaurus; shot placement is paramount here. A rifle scope with a top end of 9X to 15X makes sense, and the glare off the water will make you consider the use of a sunshade. You'll need a buddy onboard with an accurate rangefinder; odds are you'll only get one shot, so make it count. Oh, and a diver's bang-stick—12-gauge shotgun with slugs is best—would be a

The long-range accuracy of the .300 Winchester helped garner its reputation as a Plesiosaur cartridge.

great piece of kit to pack along. Should you get the Plesiosaur near the boat, hit it with the bang-stick to pay the insurance; the last thing you want is the beast to come back to life once onboard your boat.

By the way, I got a chance to look at Simon's Plesiosaur. All can say is that I hold the man in high regard for both his bravery and prowess as a hunter.

The Perfect Shot for Dinosaurs

The Massaro Brothers, circa 1878, mapping out the herds of remaining theropods.

INTRODUCTION TO CARNIVOROUS LAND DINOSAURS

By strange fortune alone, I happened to make the acquaintance of Mr. Jarrett Lane when he opened a little craft beer pub in my hometown. Though seven years my junior, I quickly found out we had a lot in common—including hunting —while we shared a pint at the corner of his now all-too-familiar bar. Imagine my surprise when he explained that his mother's maiden name was Massaro; we are —in fact—fourth cousins, tracing our lineage back to Italy. We compared notes and family stories, and the fact of the matter is that my great-grandfather Filippo Massaro, and Jarrett's great-grandfather Giacomo (Jack) Massaro, were brothers; moreover, they were not only brothers; they were also dinosaur hunters. Few family photographs remain, but the evidence is undeniable. What are the odds their descendants would be reunited half-a-world away and a full century later?

This was destiny, me a guy who loves to hunt globally, and Jarrett, a trained dinosaur expert. The torch has been handed down, and our exploits rival that of our forefathers. When it comes to the working knowledge of those dinosaur species that survive, few can rival Mr. Lane. Educated at the University of Connecticut, but denied his doctorate based on his beliefs that dinosaurs survive, Jarrett is one of the foremost experts on the carnivorous dinosaurs that remain on planet Earth. Please welcome Jarrett Lane, and his expertise:

Thanks Phil, glad to be here.
Up until a few short years ago I had only hoped my life's work would be recognized posthumously, like

If money were no object, a rifle like this Holland & Holland Royal in .600 Nitro Express would make a good choice for stopping huge dinosaurs.

Galileo's concept of heliocentrism. As a bit of an outcast in the paleological world, I've often been the butt of jokes—and more recently Internet memes—painting me as "that crazy dinosaur guy," much akin to a "flat-earther" or moon-landing denier. The truth is that years ago I discovered a very thoughtfully written series of notes amongst some heirlooms passed down from my great-grandfather. I'll admit I was skeptical of his adventures and chalked up the accounts as clever fiction, but when I recovered a perfect Tyrannosaur premaxilla tooth from a box of personal items stashed in a barn loft on my family's farmstead, I became fixated.

After re-reading his accounts, I decided to have the tooth dated. After subjecting the tooth to four types of modern radioactive dating, I had my smoking gun. Due to the nature of such dating methods, exact time frames are impossible, but each of the results dated the tooth less than five thousand years old. I knew from great-grandfather's written accounts it was less than two hundred. Before my evidence was brought up for peer review, the tooth was stolen and the journal was written off as a clever hoax.

The rest is history.

Massaro tracking a T. rex across a dry soda lakebed.

39

Phil Massaro and Jarrett Lane in their dinosaur camp, planning the next day's hunt.

You can only imagine my satisfaction when I received a call from Phil telling me the stories he heard while on a hunting trip in Australia. The local aboriginal tribes speak of a two-legged lizard capable of eating a man in a single bite. While most would have written off the stories as legend, Phil pressed further, and with a carton of Marlboros and a fifth of Kentucky bourbon as trade goods, he coerced a brave young aborigine to take him to the site of the attack. Phil was able to locate a footprint, measure it, and take a photo. The photo made its way to my inbox, and in seconds I identified it as a theropod. The size of it could mean only one thing—a Tyrannosaurus rex.

Jarrett Lane

Well, dear reader, my cousin has the story down correctly. I did find the evidence—in Australia of all places—and we have, indeed, rekindled the family quest. While the hunting of a large (or small for that matter) carnivorous dinosaur may seem woven with personal glory, please heed the caveats contained in the following chapters and realize that Jarrett and I are very fortunate to be alive, let alone writing these words. Of all the sections of this book, with the possible exception of the aquatic dinosaurs, the animals covered herein are the most likely to send you to meet your Maker. Proceed with caution, and please learn from our mistakes; the advice given herein is the culmination of decades of experience, and should set you well on your way to becoming a successful dinosaur hunter.

Deinonychus

DEINONYCHUS—THE FEATHERED RAZOR
CHAPTER 3

I was a youth, happy to be outside and happy to be following the deep bellows of our coon hound Abigail—a red bone with an exceptional nose. The scent took her across a nasty, deep bog that came with the appropriate stench of rotting vegetation. Dad had just lit the big plastic Dynalite flashlight when we heard Abigail scream. It was followed by a sound unfamiliar to my young ears, but I knew enough to realize it meant trouble. I heard Dad's sloshing footsteps, in that hurried gate he has when he means business, followed by the sound of his emptying the little Ruger Single-Six he carried for dispatching raccoons from trees.

"Get over here Now!" he shouted in that voice a father uses when his children are near danger.

I did my best to traverse the swamp. Now, soaked to the waist, I realized that a raccoon was no longer a concern and that Dad was giving the best medical attention to the hound that he could in the field.

"Take this and shoot anything—other than me—that moves. I've got to get Abigail out of here; she's cut up badly."

Though I was young, I'd been taught to handle the revolver, but the prospect of certain danger, close at hand, frightened me deeply. Dad used his shirt to bandage the faithful hound as best he could, and once he had her sewed up—there was a terrible gash across her chest that ran very deep—he sat me down and explained that we had run into a Deinonychus, a terror of the remote swamps.

The Perfect Shot for Dinosaurs

"I've only heard that scream once before, but we won't be hunting here again. We're very fortune to have made it out intact," he told me.

We never returned.

******

The Deinonychus is the bane of those huge wetlands that hold deer, waterfowl, and furbearing mammals, and while usually a shy, furtive creature, they become terrible when cornered. For, you see, the Deinonychus possesses a razor-sharp, sicklelike claw on each of its feet, which it uses to great effect, rending and tearing the flesh of an enemy like a samurai sword.

They are one of the smaller predators, standing at equal height with a grown man, with large males weighing on average around 175 pounds. The forelimbs resemble underdeveloped wings, with long, colorful, yet useless feathers, and three digits that terminate in small sharp claws, perfect for tearing the flesh of its victims for consumption. It is an agile beast, using its flexible tail as a perfect counterbalance when hunting in the swampy terrain it calls home.

THE HUNT

Pursuing a Deinonychus is a very challenging affair, with many early hunters falling victim to malaria before successfully taking their first animal. The marshlands and fenlands of the southern and eastern United States are probably your best bet; the locales will require diligent scouting. Asking questions of

Deinonychus

those who hunt in the area—without being obvious and without subjecting yourself to ridicule from the nonbelievers—will possibly help garner good information, but you'll need to rely upon the visual evidence: tracks, fallen feathers, and the kill sites of the Deinonychus. While I've seen them, and actually called one in with a predator call, I have yet to take my first, so I'm as eager as you are to do so. Calling is a smart idea—using moose calf calls or the distress call of a harried elk. A Deinonychus will come in quietly and stealthily. Be ready.

SHOT PLACEMENT

A brain shot on Deinonychus will instantly drop the beast, though the placement needs to be perfect. From the side, aim for the rear of the eye sockets; from the front, place your shot one inch above the top of the eyeballs. Safer is the heart/lung shot, placed on the forward line of the "wings," one-third up the body. Be sure to practice quick follow-up shots, as you'll want to be sure to anchor the beast quickly.

Following a wounded Deinonychus into those thick swamps is not for the faint of heart, and, remember, a Deinonychus can and will stand and look a man in the eye before attempting to rearrange his anatomy.

RIFLES FOR THE DEINONYCHUS

A Deinonychus is certainly not as difficult to kill as the larger predator dinosaurs, like the Allosaurus or the mighty *Tyrannosaurus rex,* but it still makes a worthy game animal. The medium-caliber rifles, like the 7mm and .30 calibers, will work when using heavy-for-caliber bullets, though I'd look to the premium

The Perfect Shot for Dinosaurs

Col. Townsend Whelen's namesake is just about perfect for the Deinonychus, especially using heavy 250-grain slugs.

Deinonychus

The often overlooked .338-'06 A-Square gives lots of flexibility to the hunter of medium-size dinosaurs.

Deinonychus

monometals and bonded-core bullets. A better choice would be one of the heavier bores, using bullets of 225 to 250 grains. The .338 Federal, the .338-'06 A-Square, the .338 Winchester Magnum, and the .35 Whelen are all solid choices for the Deinonychus. A hunter armed with a good 9.3x62 or .375 H&H wouldn't necessarily have too much gun, and for close work the good old .45-70 Government will certainly end the argument quickly.

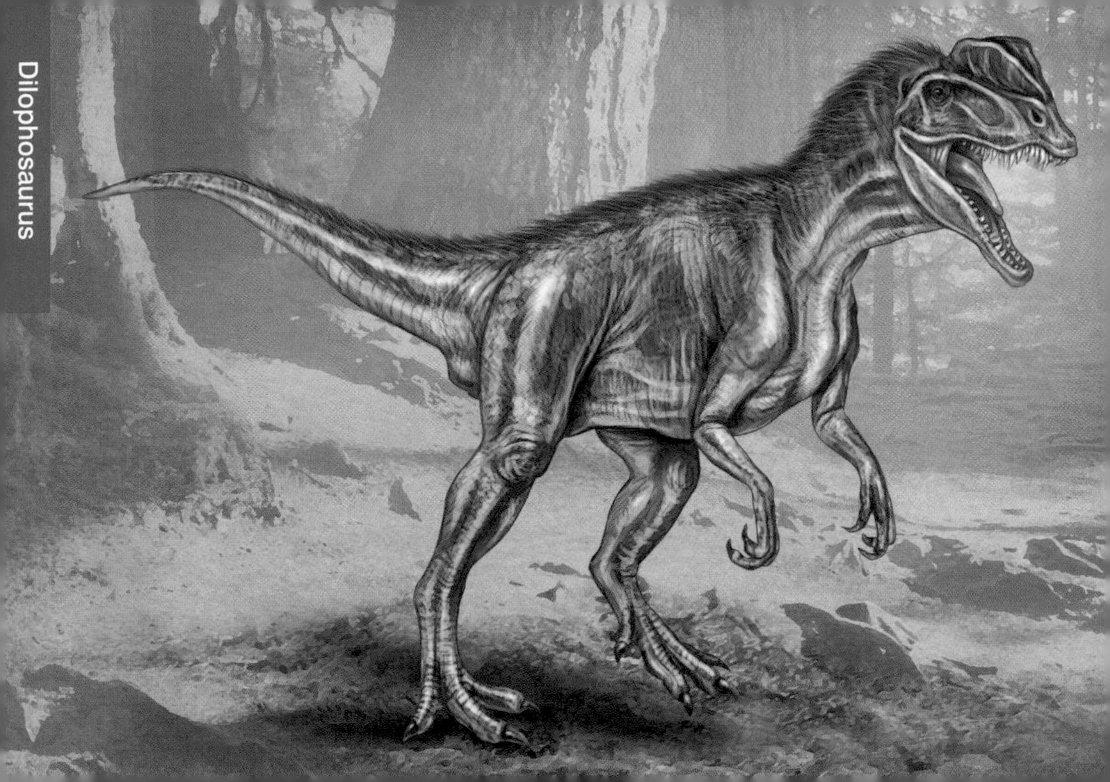

DILOPHOSAURUS—A DUAL-CRESTED TERROR
CHAPTER 4

A dear friend was fly-fishing in the mountains of northern Arizona, quietly enjoying the day in spite of tangled lines and snagged limbs. The setting was idyllic: There was a cool breeze making the pines whisper and an occasional trout feeling sorry enough for the man to take his fly. Suddenly the quiet country peace shattered. So horrendous was the squealing and thrashing sounds coming from about a hundred paces upstream that my friend nearly jumped out of his skin. In a heartbeat, tranquility vanished.

As he jerked his head toward the noise to see just what the hell was happening, the freshly lit cigar he was enjoying fell earthward, his jaw agape. A brightly colored dinosaur was jerking its jaws to swallow a huge trout whole. Terrible, needlelike teeth had severed the trophy nearly in half, and the horrible screeching and swallowing sounds caused the man to instinctively fall into the rushing water, hoping to escape notice.

His hopes were in vain, for the monster was on him in an instant, seizing him by the leg and flailing him around, much like a cat shakes a rat. His last recollection —before his head hit a boulder—was blinding pain and needing to make peace with his own mortality. He was found sometime later by hikers, alive . . . barely. The beast had hurled him through the air, and fortunately he was caught on a tree limb that kept his head above water. He was lucky to be alive, though he'll never walk right again.

The monster that maimed him was none other than a Dilophosaurus, an early theropod that generally prefers to prey on fish, but can fly off the handle like a rabid dog in the blink of an eye. No, it isn't the dinosaur portrayed in *Jurassic Park*—almost cute, until those frills extend and it spits poison—that's all Hollywood conjecture. The Dilophosaurus has no neck frills, nor a need to spit poison. It does, however, have a mouthful of sharp, thin teeth in an angled jaw that rarely releases its prey.

The twin crests on its head—Dilophosaurus translates to "two-crested-lizard"—are used in a mating display; the males are more brightly colored than the females, and much more aggressive. Standing just over six feet tall, the Dilophosaurus will use its sharp "hands" to rend flesh, making digestion a bit easier. It is a predator—perhaps not on the scale of the Tyrannosaurus—but it can and will end your life.

WHERE TO FIND THEM

The greatest concentrations of Dilophosaurs are in the high, thick forests of northern Arizona and southern Colorado. Look to the multitude of streambanks, where tracks of Dilophosaurus can be found as it feeds in the rapidly flowing streams; the tail marks between the rear feet are a telltale sign. The females tend to nest in the elk wallows within five hundred yards of the largest watercourses, and if you catch the mating season (usually September), you'll have the best crack at a trophy male. An ambush is the best hunting technique. Make sure your ambush works; otherwise, the Dilophosaurus will hunt you.

SHOT PLACEMENT

The Dilophosaurus has a long neck with ten huge vertebrae, and its physiognomy can be used to your advantage. The brain shot is an obvious choice, but in a pinch —and especially in close quarters—a

The Perfect Shot for Dinosaurs

The .470 Nitro Express will settle the fight with a Dilophosaurus quickly and effectively.

well-placed shot at the joint of neck and body will switch a Dilophosaurus to the "off" position. The heart/lung shot is another choice, but be prepared for a quick follow-up. You do not want to wound this beast. The classic Dilophosaurus reaction to a wounding is frenzied slashing at everything within its reach—and should it realize where the shot came from, you'll be cut to ribbons before you can take your next breath.

GUNS AND CARTRIDGES FOR THE DILOPHOSAURUS

Though the average weight of a trophy Dilophosaur is 850 pounds, you'll want a good, stout cartridge. They stand 10 feet tall, with an overall length of 23 feet, and are tougher than their size would indicate. I feel the sensible minimum is a 400-grain bullet with at least 2,250 fps; in other words, the .404 Jeffery, the .416

The century-plus-old .404 Jeffery when mated with modern bullets like the Woodleigh Hydro Solid becomes an even more effective cartridge.

norma

10 CARTRIDGES • 10 CARTOUCHES

AFRICAN PH

As if the .458 Lott wasn't already a great choice for the giant predators, Norma's heavy bullets in its African PH line make it even better.

Rigby, and the .416 Remington. Penetration is key, but the throw weight of the lower .40s helps the cause as well. The .458 Winchester and .458 Lott—and the .450 and .470 NE in the double rifles—offer even more stopping power, and that's paramount for a Dilophosaurus. Look to the modern, semiexpanding monometal solids like the North Fork Cup Solid and the Woodleigh Hydrostatically Stabilized Solid; both offer the consummate blend of penetration and vital tissue damage. I truly believe these two projectiles will be the future of dinosaur hunting ammunition.

Sinornithosaurus

SINORNITHOSAURUS—TERROR OF THE ORIENT
CHAPTER 5

Deep in the bamboo forests of China —in those wild places where the furtive panda bear hides—dwells a small, cunning, and unique animal: the Sinornithosaurus. Few will admit to its existence, yet those who have had the good fortune to have hunted in that remote area of the world will tell of the terror of the forest, a fright the native guides call "Niáo Xiyi." It has appeared on coins and medallions, it has been celebrated—in its hypothesized extinction—as a symbol of national pride. Once you speak to those guides, however, you'll soon realize that they know the Sinornithosaurus is not extinct but is well and truly alive.

It has, perhaps, had an influence on the Chinese dragon legends, for if you watch a brood of brightly colored Sinornithosaurs moving in a line, you'll see that it mimics the dragon rituals so inherently a part of that culture. At just over three feet long, this bird-lizard can be a menace to its surroundings, and for those people who live in the remote villages on the edge of its territory, it is a very real menace, indeed. The tales of Niáo Xiyi coming into huts, stealing children, or preying on the elderly are more than just fairy tales to these people. They all have first-hand accounts of run-ins with this so-called "extinct" dinosaur.

Its prehensile wings terminate in razor-sharp claws, and its rear feet have raptorlike talons that can open flesh like a zipper. A Sinornithosaurus can easily be mistaken for a bird, especially considering the variety of bright plumage that the birds of that part of the world are bedecked with. However, it is no peacock, and certainly no subject for a pretty picture.

Sinornithosaurus

The Niáo Xiyi may be small—when measured against an Apatosaurus or a Gorgosaurus—but it comes with a venomous bite that will cause an agonizing death within a day or two. There is more pain and suffering in the eighteen-inch tall terror than one could imagine, and though it weighs a mere seven or eight pounds, you'll think you've met a demon from Hell itself. More than one dinosaur hunter has fallen into the "bird trance," as the local Chinese call it, and passed on to the Happy Hunting Grounds. Avoid that bite at all costs.

THE HUNT FOR SINORNITHOSAURUS

Hunting in China is no mean feat, and getting there is going to be a major portion of the battle. This is one reason that the Sinornithosaurus remains high on the list of serious dinosaur hunters; it represents a level of dedication that few possess. Once there, you'll need to hire native guides to start your journey into the bamboo. The firm of Hucky & Steinherr Pty. Ltd. can, for a fee, set you up with some of the best guides in the region

SHOT PLACEMENT

As if it were a small turkey, you want to take head shots only, as the heavy feathers can and will eat up enough of the pellet's energy to result in a wounded animal, and that can spell disaster. Though only a foot-and-a-half high, the Sinornithosaurus is over three feet long, so ignore the length of creature, and concentrate on hitting the head, which will destroy the brain or break the neck.

The Perfect Shot for Dinosaurs

Sinornithosaurus

Sinornithosaurus

Good old buckshot will handle the Sinornithosaurs at close ranges.

GUNS FOR THE SINORNITHOSAURUS

I recommend a good 12-gauge shotgun, either pump or semiautomatic, loaded with 0000 buckshot, preferably in the 3-inch magnum configuration. Just like you would with a turkey, you want to take head shots only, as the heavy feathers can and will eat up enough of the pellet's energy to result in a wounded animal, and that can spell disaster.

Load that gun with as many shells as it'll hold as there may be more than one Niáo Xiyi present, and you may be forced to shoot your way out of a bamboo forest. For preparation, take your chosen shotgun—I personally prefer my well-worn Remington 870

The Perfect Shot for Dinosaurs

If properly placed, 0000 buckshot will flatten a Sinornithosaurs.

Sinornithosaurus

Sinornithosaurus

Express—to a good sporting-clays course to get in lots of practice. Concentrate on the "rabbit" style targets to sharpen your eye.

While hunting, keep your eyes on the vegetation above your head; while the Sinornithosaurus is a flightless dinosaur, it can glide for short distances and will actively do so when cornered or frightened. Keep your ears open for the high, shrill call of the Niáo Xiyi; it's a dead giveaway of their presence, and one that your Chinese guides will use to bring the Sinornithosaurus in for a close shot.

(Left) Massaro is on the hunt for a Sinornithosaurs, with his Remington shotgun fully loaded with buckshot.

Sinornithosaurus

Spinosaurus

SPINOSAURUS—GO BIG OR GO HOME
CHAPTER 6

There are theropods, and then there are theropods. While the world is enamored with the Tyrannosaurus rex—and I can understand the fixation—there are those that are larger and even more terrible. For that hunter who thrives upon the pursuit of the largest of the theropods, the Spinosaurus may well represent the pinnacle of a hunting career, for this dinosaur is nothing shy of immense. Imagine, if you will, a carnivorous beast measuring almost sixty feet in length, having the head of an appropriately scaled crocodile, standing fourteen feet tall, and weighing twenty-three tons! Yes, the Spinosaurus is the stuff of nightmares.

It is immediately identifiable because the Spinosaurus has the signature "sail" along the spinal ridge, if the sheer size weren't enough to give its species away. The sail is supported by a series of spines of up to five feet in length—of which fine walking staves are made. These are used for both mating rituals and for proper thermoregulation. Watching a male Spinosaurus ruffle his sail in the mating dance is a sight that veteran dinosaur hunters never forget, even when old age sets in and certain memories fade. The skull, which can measure nearly six feet in length in extreme cases, is highly reminiscent of the Nile crocodile, and shot placement is correlative.

The Spinosaurus walks on its rear feet, though it will belie its own size, as it walks much more horizontally than Tyrannosaurus rex and its relations. As it walks, it swings that croclike head side to side looking for prey, in both water and on land. Its widely spaced and smooth teeth act like giant war hammers, easily piercing a human skull. As you'll see, the hunt for a Spinosaurus is possibly the most dangerous in the world.

WHERE TO FIND THEM

The Spinosaurus has been pushed back to the thick bush of northern Sudan, northern Chad, and the southwest corner of Egypt, and the recent Sudanese civil war has taken its toll on these giants as well. Scavenging in these war-torn areas caused a brief increase in the Spinosaurus population as many broods of young were well fed on the gore of that war, but the devastation caused by the war also finally affected the Spinosaurs as well. Hunting in these areas—irrespective of species—is a dangerous affair, as there are still human minefields that pose a threat to life, quite separate from the threat the giant theropods pose.

Should you survive the inhospitable terrain, the Spinosaurus itself can easily end your worries; miss the shot and your chances of survival are very poor. A favored hunting method is to build a blind on the shore of a river where the water is deep; there you'll wait for the Spinosaurus to cross the water looking to feed. The head will be above water, and the beast will be slower than when on land.

SHOT PLACEMENT

Not unlike the Nile crocodile, the Spinosaurus must be hit in the brain or all your efforts will have been for naught. Miss the brain, and you'll only enrage the beast, unless you've got a Stinger missile in tow. When viewing a Spinosaurus's head from the side, look to the crease at the rear of the mouth, and come halfway up

The Perfect Shot for Dinosaurs

Spinosaurus

The penetrative qualities of the .416 Rigby are unrivaled, and the cartridge will surely handle brain shots on a Spinosaurus.

the head from that line; the brain is encased there, at the rear of the skull. The only other shot will be the Atlas joint, where the vertebrae meet the base of the skull; even then a brain shot needs to be administered to ensure the animal is dead.

If you are faced with the beast, try to time your shot so that the mouth is open, and aim for a spot about four inches above the top of the throat. That way you'll hit either the base of the brain or the spinal column. Heart shots are not recommended on unwounded Spinosaurs because of the difficulty in penetrating the huge girth and doing enough damage to incapacitate the beast.

RIFLES AND CARTRIDGES
FOR THE SPINOSAURUS

Heavy bore bullets capable of deep penetration are what you're after when attempting to hunt a Spinosaurus. As a sensible minimum, I'd recommend the .404 Jeffery, .416 Rigby, and .416 Remington, using 400-grain solid or nonexpanding bullets. The various .458s and the .470 Nitro Express with 500-

Spinosaurus

Spinosaurus

The author takes a break while tracking a big bull Spinosaurus. Midday winds tend to swirl, and you don't want a Spinosaurus to get your scent.

grain bullets are a good choice, and if the hunter can handle the recoil, cartridges like the .500 Jeffery, .500 Nitro Express, and .505 Gibbs Magnum are none too large. The .577 Nitro Express, the .577 Tyrannosaur, and the .585 Nyati are perfectly suited to the enormity that is the Spinosaurus, though I will warn you that the terrible recoil generated by these cartridges are not for the faint of heart. Be prepared to do a good amount of practice in order to shoot accurately, and precision is key when it comes to the brain shot.

The .500 Nitro Express is a smart choice for the serious Spinosaurus hunter.

Conventional solids, like the Woodleigh FMJ and the Hornady DGS, will suffice when of proper sectional density. Better are the monometal bullets, like the Barnes Banded Solid and the North Fork Solid, as there is no risk of any bullet failure. My particular favorite is the Woodleigh Hydrostatically Stabilized Solid, for it disrupts and destroys water-rich tissue by means of hydrostatic shock in addition to simple penetration. I feel it is the consummate choice for brain shots on the Spinosaurus because you'll receive a "knock-out" even if the actual brain is missed, and that allows for a follow-up shot that will anchor the behemoth.

The Perfect Shot for Dinosaurs

Spinosaurus

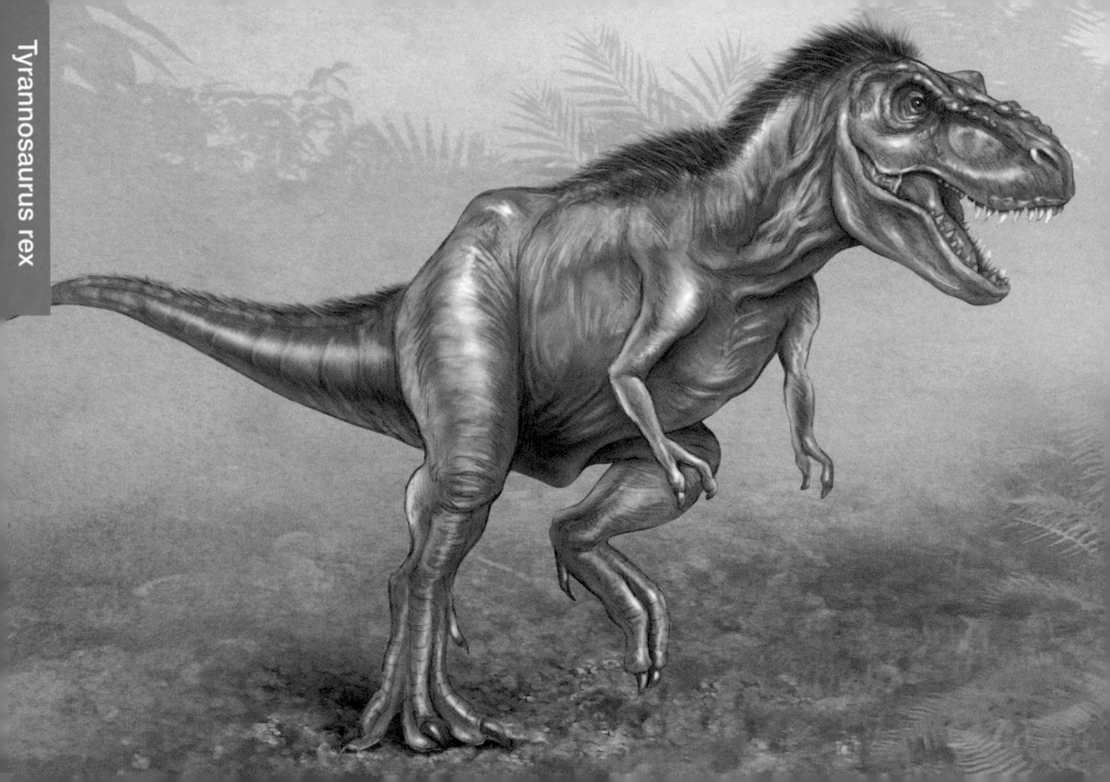

Tyrannosaurus rex

TYRANNOSAURUS REX—THE UNDISPUTED KING
CHAPTER 7

It was December of 2003 and on the return drive from a successful bison hunt in the heart of South Dakota I found myself standing in the Field Museum in Chicago, Illinois. I was there on a different agenda—I desperately wanted to see the two lions that had terrorized the Tsavo construction site in the 1890s and were neatly dispatched by Col. J. H. Patterson. Instead, I became mesmerized by the museum's main attraction. Standing in the center of the main hall is one of the greatest "discoveries" in the entire history of dinosaur science: the complete skeleton of a female Tyrannosaurus rex, the stately Sue.

As I stood there, mouth agape, I thought to myself, *It's huge, terrible, awesome*—though that word has been watered-down and cheapened, I meant it. This creature made the hair on my neck stand on end. I spent the greater part of a half-hour staring at the sheer size of the colossal beast—the teeth that would cut a man in half, the enormity of the skull, the girth of the leg bones—before I was asked to "move along."

A gentleman who was sitting on a bench while his wife was examining the northwestern Native American exhibit motioned me over and handed me his card. Written on the back was a simple phrase: "I have a T. rex you need to see." While I cannot reveal the identity of the man, suffice it to say I was in his workshop that evening.

He was more than cordial, offering me a beverage before he unveiled the specimen, a fully mature male Tyrannosaurus. It was in my examination of the skull, while looking at the eye sockets that I saw it:

a bullet hole. I've done enough examinations on dead animals to recognize the path of a bullet through bone, and it was easily apparent to those in the know. This specimen was not found, nor discovered; it was hunted.

He must have watched me come to the realization, for when I finally looked at him squarely, he simply nodded in agreement. He knew that I knew.

"You in?" he uttered.

My own nod set the wheels in motion.

Highly exploited in cinema and literature, the Tyrant King fully lives up to his reputation as a super predator. Fully equipped with all the necessary tools—including precise binocular vision, a highly developed sense of smell, and the speed and dexterity to close the deal on any prey animal—the Tyrannosaur is actually more ferocious than any scientist would purport. It can see and focus in a 55-degree range and is able to spot a future meal at distances exceeding three miles. It is a blitzkrieg incarnate, moving in violent bursts with ultimate precision. To put it layman's terms, you're dead before you know it.

It is forty feet long, stands over eighteen feet tall, and weighs somewhere in the neighborhood of eight to ten tons. It is a nightmare with teeth, and unless you yourself are attuned to the mannerisms and patterns of apex predators, you represent nothing more than an appetizer. Human beings are the hors d'oeuvres on a Tyrannosaur's menu.

The large head is perfectly counterbalanced by the thick tail, giving the T. rex the maneuverability of an all-pro running back. The forelimbs that have been ridiculed for generations act as landing gear on a warplane,

The Perfect Shot for Dinosaurs

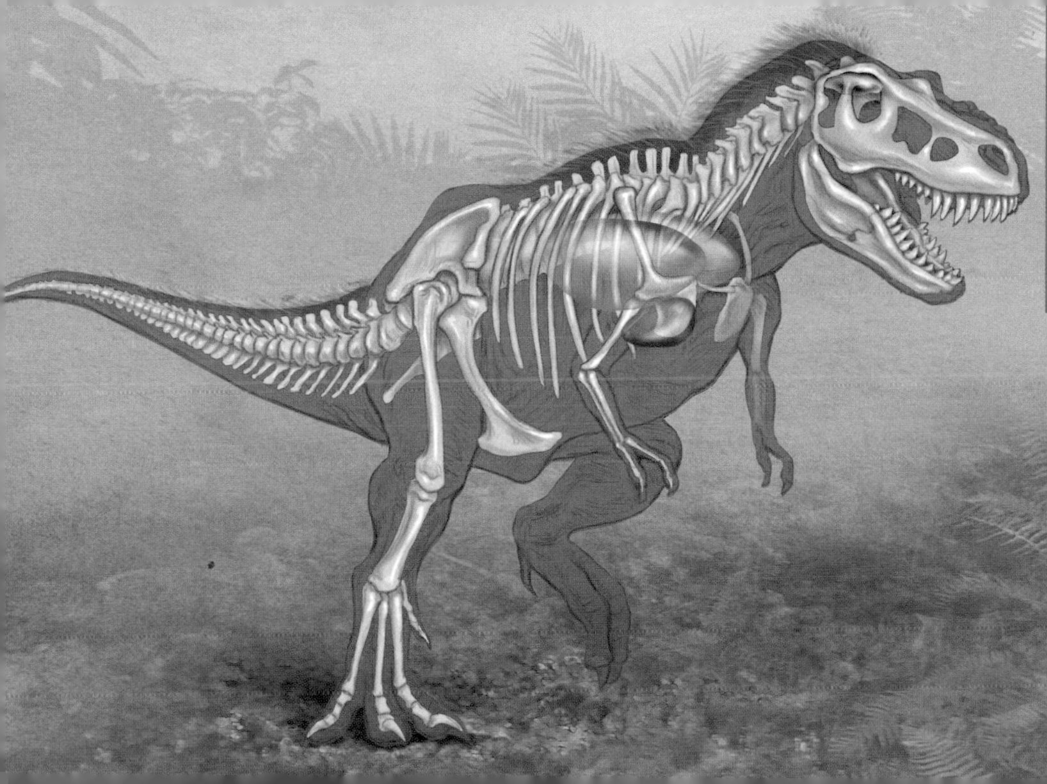

steadying the beast as it feeds upon the carcass of anything it fancies. And those feet! Filled with elastic ligaments holding together a three-toed skeletal system, the Tyrant King will dig in for purchase with its ferocious head extended, attaining speeds in excess of twenty-five miles per hour when it means business. The Tyrannosaurus rex is the perfect predatory package. Truly.

Want a really good bolt gun for hunting a T. rex? Look long and hard at the .505 Gibbs Magnum!

WHERE TO FIND THEM

I was in Arnhem Land, Northern Territory, Australia, under the guise of a water buffalo hunt with none other than my friend Chris Sells of Heym USA. Chris and I have made several safaris together and had become good friends over the years; we share a

The Perfect Shot for Dinosaurs

passion for dangerous game rifles, both bolt-action and double rifles. We had taken a couple of buffaloes, and during our travels across the twelve-million-acre concession we had had the opportunity to see what makes the Northern Territory tick.

To be brief, we got lost one night and had to navigate by compass and stars. While looking for a crossing at a small river, Sells and I saw a mystifying sight: the fresh tracks of a juvenile T. rex. We were asked to immediately "get the hell back in the car," and needless to say, our hunting focus changed the next day. Yes, dear reader, the Aussie wilds are the haunts of the Tyrannosaur. It was where I took my first T. rex—though the Australian authorities have confiscated my photos—and where I will return for any future Tyrannosaurus hunting. There are sparse populations in the Javanese jungles, but the Australian populations are the most prevalent.

HUNTING THE TYRANNOSAUR

Like the African lion and leopard, a T. rex must be baited in order to give a hunter even the slightest chance. However, these beasts prefer to catch their prey themselves, only scavenging when hard times fall. I suggest the largest piece of meat you can find—water buffalo in the hot sun will suffice; I also suggest practicing the sounds of a wounded specimen.

In a double rifle, the .500 Nitro Express may represent the best balance of striking power and tolerable recoil.

The Perfect Shot for Dinosaurs

A hurried photo, just as the author draws down on a Tyrannosaur.

Tyrannosaurus rex

I consulted my dear friend and cousin Jarrett Lane—and his vast bank of dinosaur hunting knowledge—to shed some light on the actual body functions of the Tyrant King. I'll allow him to expound….

> Paleontologists debate whether the T. rex of the ancient world was a pack hunter or whether it shared its kills with family and group members. Regardless, the contemporary Tyrannosaur exhibits none of that decorum. In fact, they have been witnessed in the wild exhibiting behaviors that at first glance seem counterintuitive to their long-term survival. These behaviors include cannibalism, infanticide, sport killing, and the violent defense of hunting grounds far too large to be effectively enforced by one territorial theropod. With the exception of the mating season, a T. rex will view any living vertebrate, even another T. rex, as either food or a competition for resources. You, the hunter, are no exception.
>
> Most common reptiles like the American alligator are ectothermic, or more colloquially "cold blooded." Ectotherms

Richard, my guide in Arnhem Land, Australia, showed me my first Tyrannosaurus rex.

The Perfect Shot for Dinosaurs

81

While the .458 Lott is a well-respecte[d]
cartridge, it is only marginal for th[e]
Tyrant King.

maintain metabolic rates from external temperatures and tend to spend a lot of time in warm-weather environments sunning themselves. As the mercury dips, alligators become more sluggish. As the temperature rises, they become more active.

Endothermic or "warm blooded" animals like mammals and birds represent the other end of the spectrum. This endothermic type of metabolic regulation allows for quicker muscular response and general reflex. While endotherms are considered to have the more evolved metabolic system, each has advantages, namely speed and endurance for endotherms and an overall robustness for ectotherms.

The Tyrannosaurus rex is nature's perfect hybrid, a true mesotherm. Its system is internally regulated, but also supplemented by the sun. Because of this unique mesothermic metabolic system, the T. rex has the burst speed and endurance of a large mammal while maintaining the toughness and feeding cycles of a Nile crocodile. The T. rex will gorge itself and digest in hiding for days or even weeks on end. This is widely speculated to be the reason why such an enormous predator's existence has remained little more than a myth for eons.

The average modern T. rex is a scaled-down version of the fossilized remains you may have gawked over as a child. This is due to a number of factors ranging from reduced atmospheric oxygen levels to extra-species competition for resources, but every once in a while a monster emerges that is every bit the size of its Cretaceous ancestors. An animal like this requires hundreds of pounds of fresh meat per week and is capable of wiping a ranch clean of cattle in a matter of months. Throughout modern times ranchers have awoken to fields of slaughtered cows and goats. These attacks have spawned a menagerie of speculation that blamed everything from alien attacks to the actions of satanic cults. In reality, these encounters are most likely the territorial killings of a roaming T. rex.

The Perfect Shot for Dinosaurs

The .500 Jeffery is a beast of a cartridge, well-suited to the Tyrant King.

Thank you Jarrett, I've seen your expertise at work in the field, and I truly appreciate the insight. So folks, you'll need to cover any and all human scent in order to fool the olfactory senses of these great predators, and it's one of the few instances where head-to-toe camo is warranted. Work the wind, and let that meat create all the stink you can, for you've got to fool the smartest predator ever to grace planet Earth.

SHOT PLACEMENT

Brain shots are the way to go with the T. rex. That's the only real shot you've got—and you'll only get one shot. Body shots on a Tyrannosaur will—in time—kill the beast, but I guarantee you'll die first.

RIFLES FOR THE TYRANNOSAUR

Make no mistake about it: You want the biggest stick you can shoot accurately to take down a T. rex. Should you have the misfortune of wounding a Tyrannosaurus, I highly doubt you'll live to tell the tale.

The Perfect Shot for Dinosaurs

Think about the rifles that are appropriate for the professional hunter who specializes in hunting elephants in really thick vegetation where immediate knockdown power and penetration are paramount.

Stay away from any rifles below .500 caliber. Even my beloved .470 Nitro Express is marginal when it comes to that huge skull since your bullet must reach the brain. The .500 NE, the .577 NE, and .600 NE are excellent in the double-rifle category, and the .500 Jeffery, .505 Gibbs, .577 Tyrannosaur (hello?!?), and .585 Nyati are solid choices for the bolt-gun class. All should be loaded with the heaviest monometal, nonexpanding solids for the particular caliber.

As a bit of trivia that few may be aware of, it was the 2017 Australian hunt that prompted Chris Sells to chamber the famous Heym Express by Martini in the .505 Gibbs cartridge; we decided on that configuration as a Tyrannosaur rifle first and foremost.

The Perfect Shot for Dinosaurs

INTRODUCTION TO THE FLYING DINOSAURS

Since man has been cognizant enough to be aware of his surroundings, he has marveled at the mystery of flight, and I feel confident in saying that the flying dinosaurs played a big role in that admiration. The largest of those dinosaurs to first take flight—with their outlandish beaks capable of skewering a grown *Homo sapiens*—surely caused panic in early man, as they do in modern man. All of our understanding, all of our scientific knowledge, and all of the bravery we can muster will often crumble to dust when we look skyward and see the sun blotted out by a Pteranodon. Instincts are instincts, and our *Homo sapiens* forefathers were undoubtedly wise enough to have feared and avoided death from above . . . as should we be.

Not unlike the dragons of old, the Pteranodon is a fierce opponent in battle. There were and are those brave enough to face the beast, and to do their best to kill it. I can picture our earliest ancestors, developing first the spear and then the bow, as a means of bringing down a beast from above.

One of the keys to man's success is his embrace of technology and tools to replace his weak fangs, tiny nails, and small frame. Only through the advancement of tools has man been able to level the playing field in nature. Today's shotguns and rifles get the job done much better than sticks, stones, spears, and bows. What has not advanced, however, is freedom from fear. That factor is still there, for certain. A hunt against a Pteranodon is no day in the duck blind, no spring jaunt in hopes of a tom turkey; this is a fight that could mean your life, and you had damned well better take it seriously.

The smaller flying dinosaurs, like the brightly feathered Archaeopteryx, do not pose the threat that the largest beasts do, but can still turn the tables when wounded, putting both hunter and dog at risk. These flying reptiles may look like birds, but . . . use your head and be sure to use enough gun.

Archaeopteryx

ARCHAEOPTERYX—CHICKEN WINGS, JURASSIC STYLE
CHAPTER 8

I was on my first driven hunt—in Poland, just east of the German border—and enjoying the various European game species that came boiling out of the forest ahead of the beaters and dogs. Wild boar, roe deer, foxes, badgers, and red stags were all on the menu. Then there were the varieties of birds. Ah, paradise.

It was the third beat of the morning, and I'd already taken a big *keiler*, or mature wild boar, when I heard one of the dogs yelp. I looked up just in time to see a brightly colored bird gliding overhead, high and just to my right.

My wife, Suzie, who was running a video camera for me, turned to me with an honestly stunned expression and said, "What the *hell* was that?!?"

Our astonished attention was directed earthward toward the dog now squealing in pain. Rushing over to where he lay, we saw that he had a nasty gash across his chest. He was obviously in pain, so we bundled him up and got him to a veterinarian to be stitched up.

After I started to put the scenario together, I couldn't help but wonder at what we had seen. If my suspicions were correct, the rest of the group needed to be kept in the dark, for I had no wish to cause panic. It took a bit of translating as my Polish is terrible, but I soon befriended a veteran Polish hunter named Lukasz. My hope was to pump him for information.

His tongue now adequately lubricated by an appropriate dose of Żubrówka Vodka, also known as Bison Grass Vodka, Lukasz exclaimed, *"Starozytny ptak, Dárz bor!"* The rough translation of this is, "Very old bird." Several bar napkins were employed for a drawing board, and I soon realized I had seen my first Archaeopteryx, the bridge between dinosaurs and the later evolution of birds. We hastily reviewed the video that Suzie had taken, but her fear had gotten the best of her. The best view we could salvage from the video was an up-close-and personal look at the ground.

The Archaeopteryx is not a big dinosaur—though if that Polish hound could talk, he would testify that it can still slice and dice extremely well—but it holds a special place in the history of flight. While incapable of true flight, as we know it, the Archaeopteryx is capable of gliding to catch its prey. Its bright feathers are a trademark of the species. They are about the size of a common raven, weigh just a couple of pounds, and measure less than two feet long.

WHERE TO FIND THEM

The greatest opportunity to hunt an Archaeopteryx is in Central Europe, predominately southern Germany and Poland, though the Polish authorities take a dim view of hunters trying to bag one of these trophies. While the authorities hands are tied and cannot ban the hunt as illegal because the existence of the species is deemed "highly classified," they definitely frown upon the practice.

The Archaeopteryx prefer thick evergreen forests, and the more remote the better. They are a bit smaller than our American turkeys and are equally as cunning. They prefer to haunt the valleys, especially

The Perfect Shot for Dinosaurs

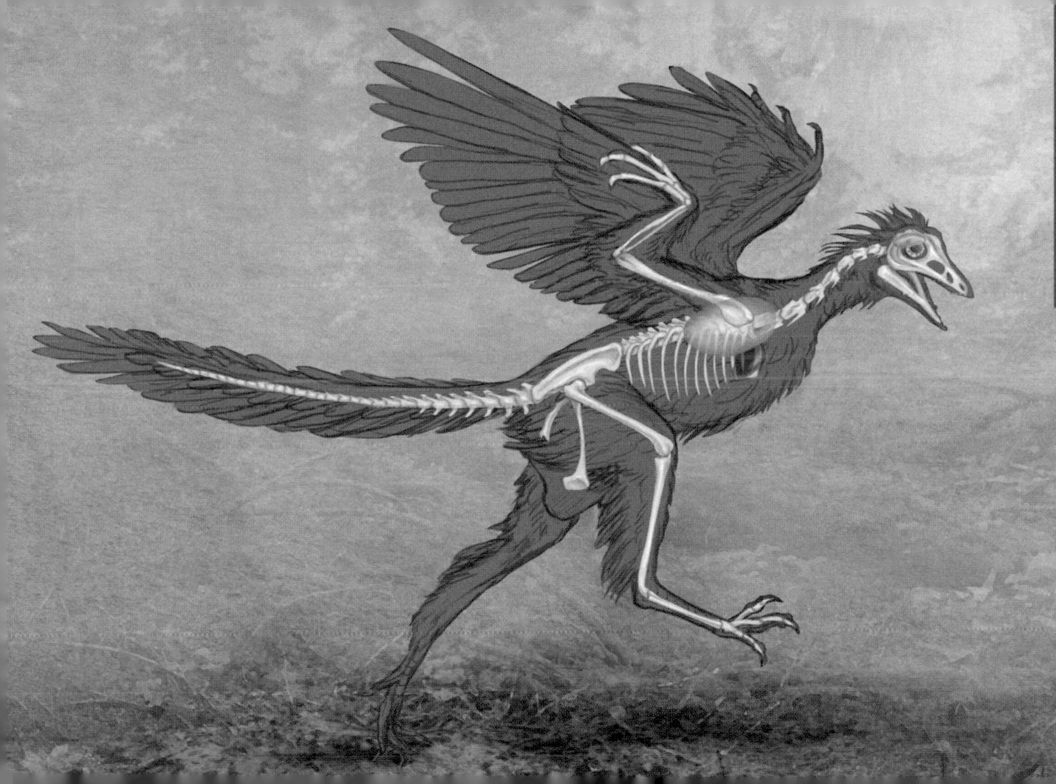

Archaeopteryx

near the numerous large streams and small rivers of that area, using the numerous trees as a launching point for their gliding as they hunt up and down in the valleys.

SHOT PLACEMENT

When using a shotgun, the shot placement is the same for any other bird; you want the center of the pattern to strike the head/neck area. Should you be using a light rifle for a flighted Archaeopteryx, aim for the center mass; the hydraulic shock will certainly kill quickly.

FIREARMS FOR THE ARCHAEOPTERYX

A shotgun makes the most sense for taking these "birds," and you'll want a gun with a bit of reach. My dear friend Shawn Skipper, who was my online editor at the NRA's *American Hunter* for years and is an accomplished shotgunner, prefers the bigger shotguns designed for distant geese and other waterfowl.

"You'll want to deliver a heavy load of large shot because you definitely do not want to wound an Archaeopteryx. I like a 12-gauge Benelli or Beretta, 3½-inch semiauto. Look to modern shot designs like Federal's Black Cloud or Prairie Storm; they'll drop a "bird" quickly and give you the quick second and third shot should you need it," Skipper instructed.

I personally prefer a classic European drilling—a side-by-side shotgun with a rifle barrel underneath—as it gives the shooter an option. If the Archaeopteryx is gliding, the shotgun may be

The Perfect Shot for Dinosaurs

employed. Yet if you happen upon a roosted Archaeopteryx, or should the creature light on a distant branch or even on the ground, a sweet-shooting rifle cartridge—like the 6.5x55 SE or 7x57 Mauser—can be employed for a precise shot, increasing not only your chances, but the distances at which the Archaeopteryx may be shot.

And yes—if you're wondering—a properly prepared Archaeopteryx makes good table fare. Expect a flavor with elements of both wild salmon and the finest mallard.

The Perfect Shot for Dinosaurs

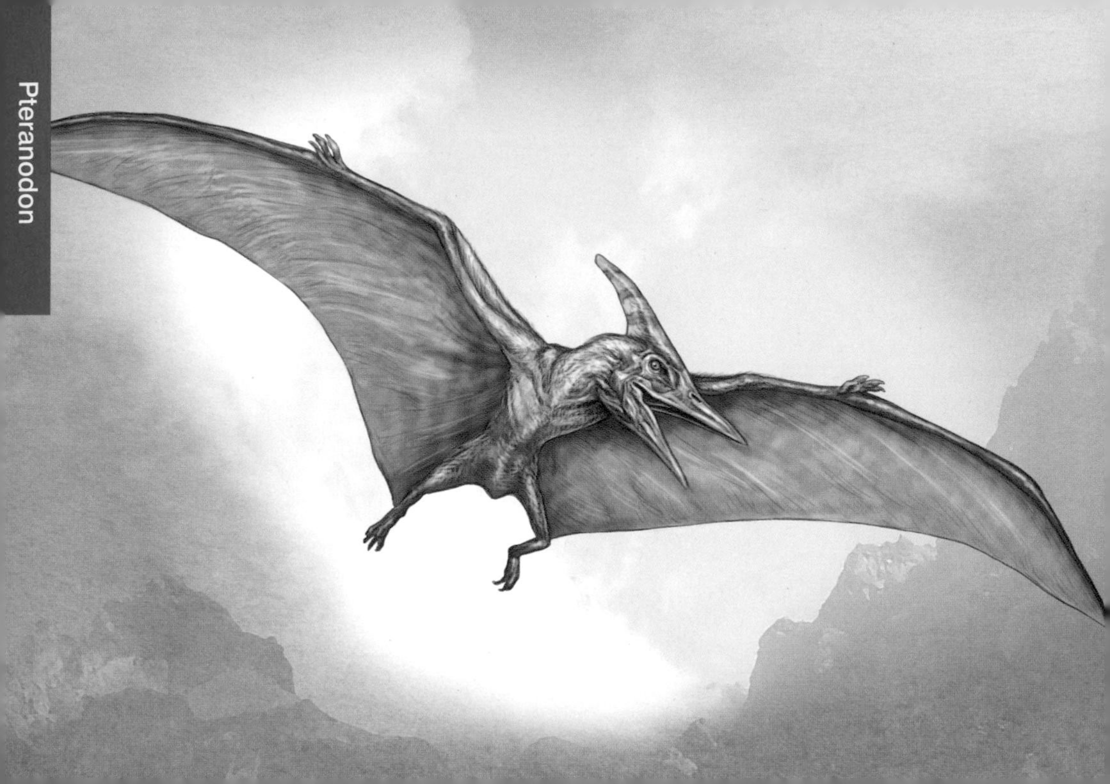

PTERANODON—DEATH FROM ABOVE
CHAPTER 9

I was bird hunting at a rather prestigious gun club in southeastern Kansas—feeling completely out of my league as a shotgunner—when Lucy, a setter with a fantastic nose, flushed a covey of quail. Miraculously, I brought the Remington automatic to shoulder and neatly took two birds with two shots, watching the second tumble violently forty yards away and into a thorn-tangled valley.

I commanded that faithful dog to retrieve the bird, and she diligently made a beeline into the thicket. All at once we heard the dog let out one helluva yelp, followed by the unmistakable sound of huge, flushing wings. While my experience with Western birds is admittedly limited, I knew that the creature producing a sound of that magnitude had to be larger than the largest turkey. The sheer volume of air being moved suggested a bellows of medieval proportions. I then witnessed, mouth agape, two huge winged shapes, one nearly twice the size of the other, sailing down into that thick valley.

Thinking I may have just witnessed a Pteranodon in motion yet not wanting to appear nosy, I decided to act ignorant as I interrogated the dog handler. Being stupid has its advantages, so I suggested to the handler that a golden eagle had attacked the dog, giving him an out if he wanted one.

"Uh, yeah. Golden eagle," he muttered.

That was all I could get out of him on the matter. Later, comfortably situated in the first-class lodge for libations, I found that the owner of the prestigious establishment—let's call him Jim, for anonymity's sake—shared my passion for fine bourbon as well as my predisposition for the volume consumed. As the other hunters bowed out, wishing the few who remained a good evening, Jim began to show the effects of the mental lubricant, and I knew the time had come to broach the topic of what I'd seen earlier that day.

"Got my first quail today, and just after my shot, I saw something very strange . . .," I began.

I was immediately cut off by a change in Jim's expression, from jovial to deadpan.

"I know you brought this up with your guide, but he isn't allowed to discuss it," Jim said. "I say that so you won't think ill of him. Lucy is a good girl, and a brave dog, but she knows better than to mess with *them*."

Feigning ignorance seemed a good strategy so as to keep my theory—a fantastic one, I admit— to myself for the present, so I innocently asked, "Will an eagle of that size kill your dogs?" I knew full well that those giant wings had not come from an eagle.

Jim motioned toward the bar for another round of neat Blanton's, and looked me squarely in the eyes. "Before you were invited here, we did our homework, and we are aware of what you've seen and what you've hunted. Let's stop pretending. We both know that those were a pair of Pteranodons, and yes, they've killed our dogs. They've also killed our calves and lambs."

The Blanton's arrived, and I forced myself to sip calmly. I was doing my best not to become overzealous, for I did not want the conversation to end prematurely.

"We see them from time to time—though less than when I was a boy," Jim said. "They can be a real danger. You see them again tomorrow, shoot them. They're terrible for business."

The Perfect Shot for Dinosaurs

Jim then added that a few rounds of buckshot would be made available before the morning hunt, and pleaded that I keep the information to myself, to which I agreed completely.

THE HUNT

The Pteranodon family includes the famous Pterodactyl, those winged terrors with their sharp, bony, toothless beaks and incredible wingspans. Though sightings are rare, they prefer flatter areas on either edge of what was—eons ago—a large, inland sea that submerged much of the Great Plains. More prevalent on the western shore of the former sea, Pterodactyls can still be found as mating pairs in Kansas and Nebraska, where I had my first sighting.

Often confused with the largest raptors, the Pteranodon will feed on stock animals, as well as coyotes, foxes, and deer. Look to signs of their feeding on winter-killed animals or the young born each spring. Scour the area. They have fantastic eyesight, so it's a difficult hunt—I've yet to get a clean shot at one—and what you'll probably see is the silhouette sailing just above the vegetation. The males are nearly twice the size of the females, though either species makes a fine trophy.

SHOT PLACEMENT

A Pteranodon will weigh between fifty and two hundred pounds—again the drastic difference between the males and females—with a wingspan topping out at eighteen feet in some cases, and they can stand

The Perfect Shot for Dinosaurs

six feet tall. Be prepared for an instinctual cringing; it has been programmed in our DNA to fear flying beasts of this magnitude. That huge beak needs to be ignored when swinging on a Pteranodon; you want to break the joint where the skull meets the neck.

GUNS FOR THE PTERANODON

You'll definitely want a shotgun, with a decent payload of heavy shot. A double barrel offers no disadvantage to the pumps or autoloaders, as one or two shots is more than likely all you're going to get anyway. I prefer a sweet handling over/under, as it is quicker to shoulder and seems to balance a bit better. I like No. 4 Buckshot as it provides a good pattern and can bring the big creatures down quickly.

Finer shot sizes can be used, though I feel No. 2 shot is as small a shot size as one should employ. In addition, based on Jim's experiences and advice, I carry two or three slugs in my pocket in case I wing a Pteranodon and need to finish it off on the ground. They can use that beak to chilling effect, and you want to finish it quickly, without destroying the trophy beak.

Quetzalcoatlus

QUETZALCOATLUS—A WINGED NIGHTMARE
CHAPTER 10

I was following Jay Leyendecker—a fantastic professional hunter—on the tracks of a huge aoudad in South Texas when the bright blue sky uncannily darkened. We instinctively looked skyward thinking a violent storm had overtaken us and we might be in danger of being caught in a tornado. When I saw the huge wingspan, coupled with a beak that resembled something out of a nightmare, I fell earthward and remained absolutely motionless.

"Stay down," Leyendecker instructed, "you're about to see something incredible."

It wasn't one, but two gigantic winged beasts—huge, terrible, and yet beautiful simultaneously. They swooped, they glided, and when they beat their wings it produced a sound I'll never forget.

"Quetzalcoatlus," Leyendecker whispered, "a mating pair. Don't move a muscle."

We were dressed in camouflage, so we were perfectly hidden, which allowed us to witness the mating dance of two of the most fantastic Pterosaurs ever to grace the Earth. Once landed, their necks began to intertwine, and high-pitched shrieks emanated from horrifying beaks. The entire affair lasted less than a minute, but it was a spectacular thing to see—a flying monster in finely feathered garb, switching from dragonlike flight to a hideous quadruped once on terra firma. And that beak! It could skewer a grown man in much the same way we skewer shrimp for a barbecue.

The Quetzalcoatlus is named for the feathered serpent god of the Mayans, and with one look it's easy to understand why. If ever the mythical dragon was incarnate, it is likely as not the huge Quetzalcoatlus.

The Perfect Shot for Dinosaurs

Quetzalcoatlus

With a wingspan approaching forty-five feet on an adult male, these huge flying predators are the terror of the skies. Though sightings are rare, there are huntable numbers, especially throughout southern Texas and northern Mexico.

THE HUNT

The hunt itself is a rather unorthodox affair, as it will be a combination of glassing and tracking. Tracks are most easily found along the watercourses. Look for tracks of the rear feet that make a normal track along with the stunted "feet" that protrude from the joint in the wing. The two, small additional feet allow for quadrupedal movement on the ground; note that the front "stunted" feet will be turned significantly inward. Once tracks are found and presence confirmed, obtaining a high vantage point in the rocky hills above the watercourse allows the hunter and guide to glass the vast terrain, looking for movement at first and last light. Being a predator, the Quetzalcoatlus can be decoyed, baited, or lured. If you have an experienced guide, this largest flying animal of all time may even be called into an ambush.

SHOT PLACEMENT

Aim for the wing/body joint, where the "shoulder" would be, and you'll get the top of the heart and lungs. For the brain shot, hold just at the rear of the head, level with the eye socket, and you should drop that huge reptile in its tracks.

Quetzalcoatlus

The Perfect Shot for Dinosaurs

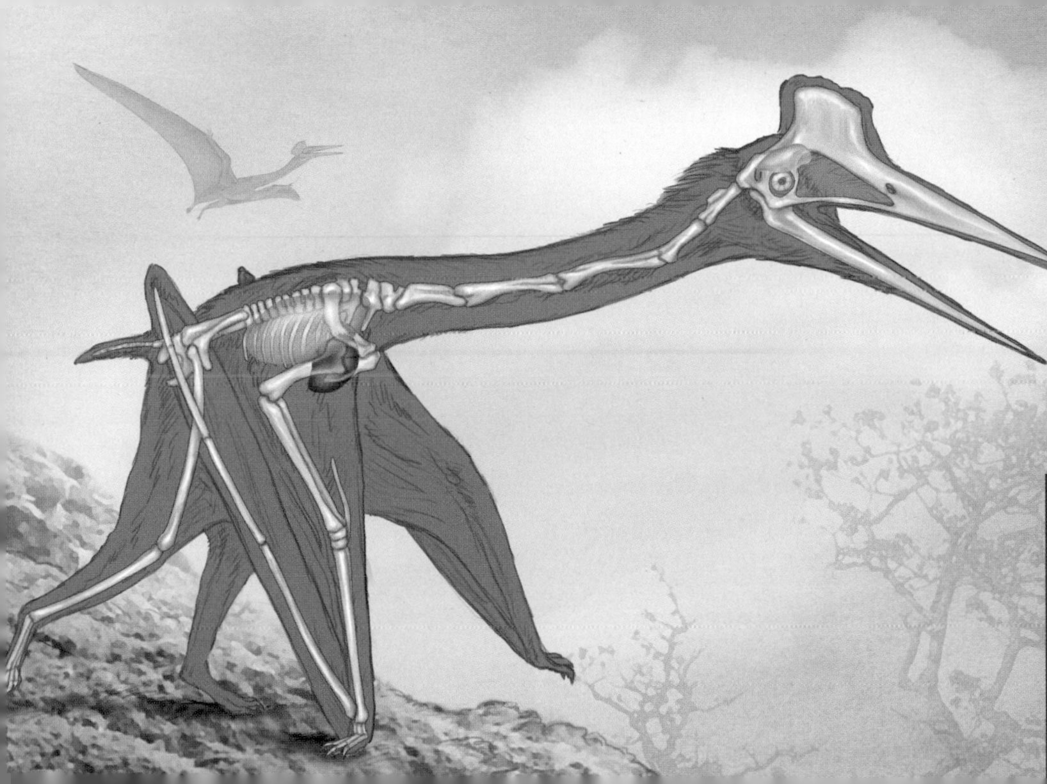

Quetzalcoatlus

Otto Bock's 9.3x62 Mauser is a light-recoiling, hard-hitting rifle, perfectly capable of cleanly taking a Quetzalcoatlus.

GUNS FOR THE QUETZALCOATLUS

Taking a Quetzalcoatlus is a bit different from taking any of the other winged creatures on the planet. Females will weigh between 380 and 425 pounds, with the larger males tipping the scales at 400 to 550 pounds, so both genders require a serious firearm. I prefer a 3½-inch 10-gauge, delivering 18 pellets of 00 buckshot. However, the shotgun is only half of the equation.

If one of these large pterosaurs is on the ground, they can be taken within 100 yards with a good medium-bore

The Perfect Shot for Dinosaurs

The beauty of the .375 Holland & Holland Belted Magnum is that it can handle nearly anything, including the Quetzalcoatlus.

The Perfect Shot for Dinosaurs

Quetzalcoatlus

AMMUNITION

Nosler Custom
HANDLOADED AMMUNITION

Custom Loaded for
Phil Massaro

375 H&H Mag
260gr. AccuBond
2750 FPS
20 Rounds

Quetzalcoatus

rifle such as the 9.3x62 or 9.3x74. The good old .375 H&H will also work. One of the modern bolt-action rifles chambered for any decent dangerous-game cartridge, topped with a good, low-power scope will get the job done. Only premium softpoints such as the Swift A-Frame, Woodleigh Weldcore, Barnes TSX, and Peregrine Bushmaster should be used, for you'll have to penetrate thick muscles on the body shots.

A drilling of good lineage, offering a shotgun barrel of at least 12-gauge, and a pair of rifle barrels of no less than 9.3mm caliber, driving a premium bullet of 250 grains to 300 grains would make a good choice for the hunter who has a Quetzalcoatlus high on his or her list.

(Left) Massaro's favorite .375 H&H load for Quetzalcoatlus is custom loaded by Nosler and features the 260-grain AccuBond bullet.

Quetzalcoatlus

PH Poen van Zyl and
Massaro (right), gathe.
intelligence in an Afri
village as they prepare f
dino hunt.

INTRODUCTION TO HERBIVOROUS DINOSAURS

While the ferocious predators get all the glory, great sport can be had when pursuing the many different species of herbivores in the dinosaur world. From the easily recognizable Triceratops, to the sheer might of the Brachiosaurus, to the armored Stegosaurs and Ankylosaurus, there is plenty of action up and down the size scale. Remember, where there are prey animals (the herbivores), there will also be predators, and I'm not just talking about us humans.

As if the clubbed tails, enormous horns, various spiked frills, et al., weren't enough to deal with, you need to realize that the herbivorous dinosaurs are herd animals, and that means they are a draw for the terrible carnivores. In the same fashion as the great game mammals that congregate in herds, there are countless numbers of eyes, ears, and noses that need to be fooled and outsmarted.

You'll need to be in good shape, as many of these giants are located in some of the most remote and hostile territory you may ever encounter. However, that's the name of the game; we are the tiny, near-hairless conquerors of the world, and we need to use all of the skills and technological developments to maintain our dominance under the environmental conditions where the dinosaur still reigns supreme.

As a hunter, the danger is two-fold: First of all, it is difficult enough to take one of the herbivores from its herd, and that alone presents a special set of challenges. Yet, during the post-shot elation, you need also to realize that the tremendous amounts of blood, guts, and hide that will be present during the field-dressing and butchering will—most definitely—attract the scavengers and predators, and that is where

A vintage John Rigby & Co. in .500 Nitro, designed for hunting the Stegosaurs.

things can get sticky. Keep your head about you, be sure to shoot straight, and be wary when preparing your trophies in the field.

Few, if any, will be able to complete the "Herbivore Slam," as there is confusion and conjecture regarding which species actually survive, and of those, which have a huntable population. Hunting any dinosaur is a ticklish subject, as there are no game laws to cover it. I do, however, know of hunters who've ended up in serious legal hot water as a result of taking something as plentiful as a Gallimimus. Please, err on the side of caution, or at least plan to keep your attorney's cell number handy.

Ankylosaurus

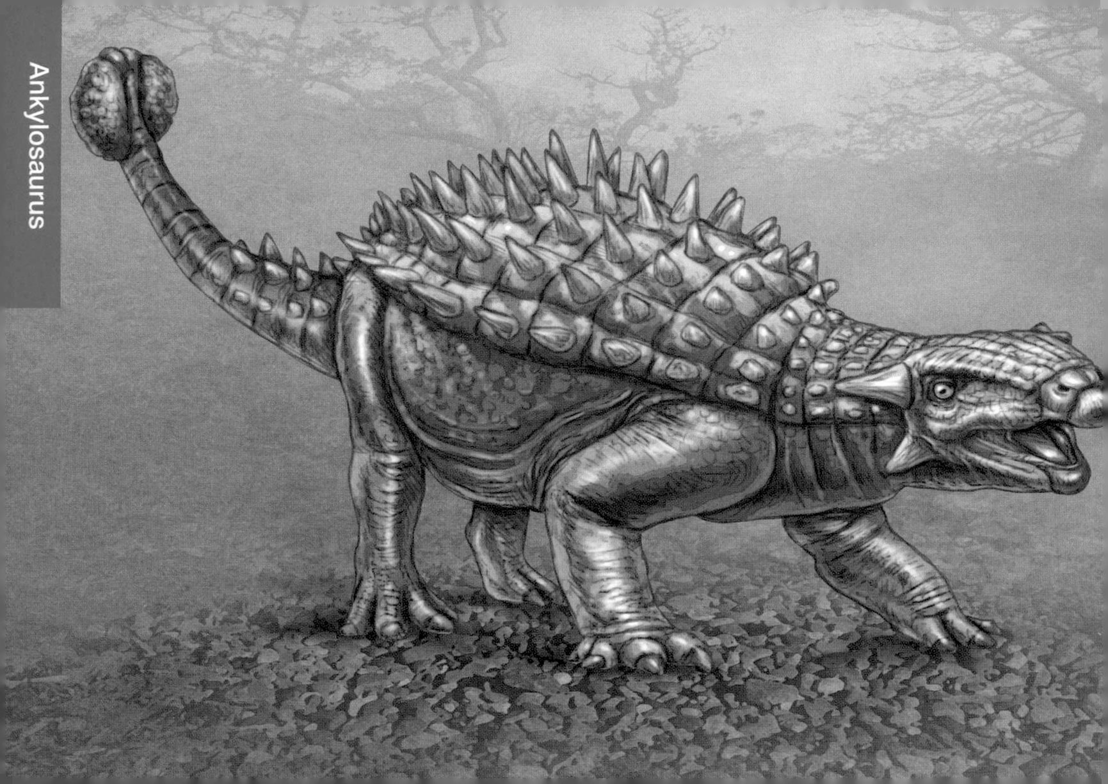

ANKYLOSAURUS—A LIVING TANK
CHAPTER 11

Deep in the Montana wilds, among the favorite haunts of elk, moose, and grizzly bear, a hunter who has fortune on his or her side may catch a glimpse of Ankylosaurus, the armored dinosaur. You yourself may have seen one—if you traverse that area of Montana where the largest concentrations are—though you may not have recognized it.

An Ankylosaurus can measure up to thirty-five feet long, including the tail, though it stands just over five feet tall. It can weigh over seven tons. Armored in knobby plates, covering the entire upper portion of the body, the ruddy brown tone of the Ankylosaurus will blend in very well with its surroundings, looking very much like a rock formation if it remains perfectly still. I've spent countless hours glassing for them, and I can't tell you how many times I've simply looked right past them. But, once you see your first, you'll become intrigued with this armored car of the dinosaurs.

THE HUNT

Hunting an Ankylosaurus is a combination tracking/glassing hunt. They are slow movers, feeding peacefully, but you must be patient in the pursuit. They have a great sense of smell, so make sure of wind direction for a successful stalk. An interesting tidbit is that the nostrils on an Ankylosaurus point

The .458 Winchester Magnum offers the energy and penetration required to anchor the Ankylosaurus.

sideways instead of forward. Know that an Ankylosaur will just as soon turn to fight as try to evade. Their huge clubbed tail, capable of crushing a man with a single blow, can and will be used to good effect.

Look for trees with excessive amounts of bark stripped away; this is a favorite food of the Ankylosaurus and indicative of their presence. Unlike other species of dinosaurs, the Ankylosaur is a loner, avoiding congregation with the exception of during the mating season.

Once your shot is placed, be very wary during the follow up. A wounded Ankylosaur will remain motionless until it is aware of the close presence of the predator, and then the excrement will hit the oscillator. The clubbed tail will flail, and those terrible horns at the rear of the skull were designed to rearrange your anatomy with certainty. Pay the insurance shot, no matter what. To judge a trophy Ankylosaurus, look for a wide skull, worn horn tips, and a thick, fully developed tail club.

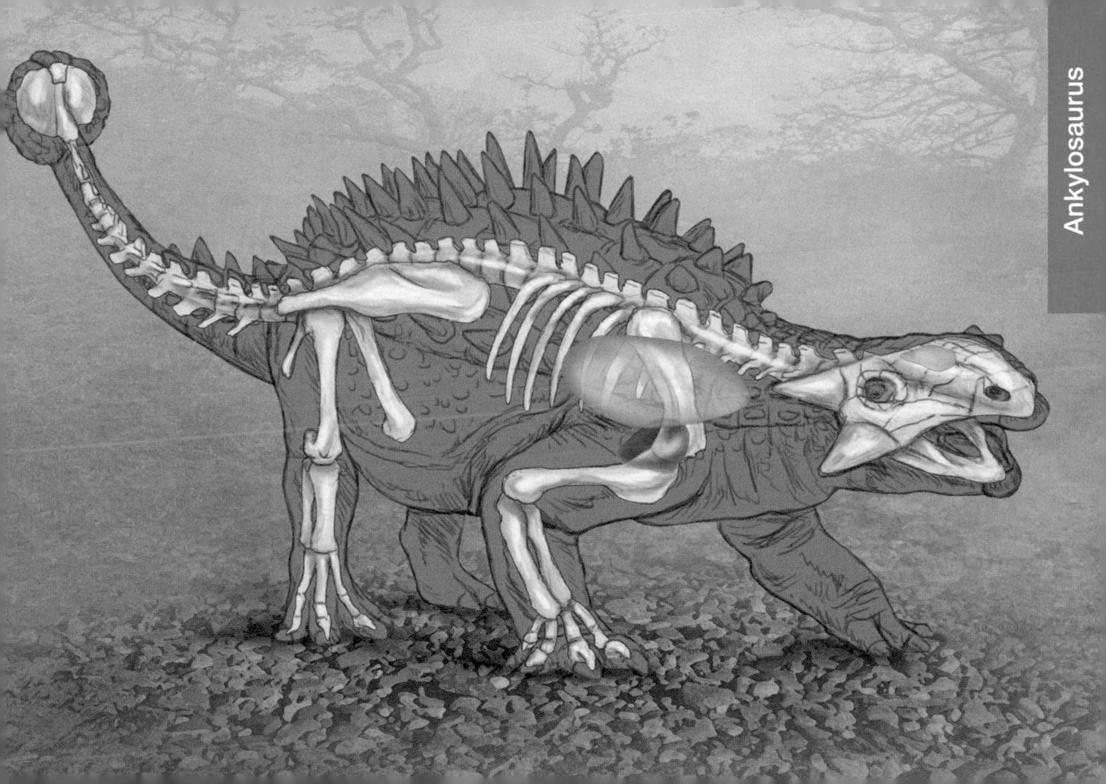

One of the author's favorite herbivore rifles: a Winchester Model 70 in .416 Remington Magnum.

SHOT PLACEMENT

An Ankylosaur is well-equipped for protection from any and all predators, including modern man and the fantastic lineup of cartridges and firearms we've developed. Those knobby plates that cover the back, neck, and tail are extremely difficult to penetrate and will deflect even the heavy-for-caliber monometal solids, if the shot angle is wrong.

The bones of the Ankylosaur's skull are fused together, making a brain shot a tricky affair, so knowing the anatomy of the Ankylosaurus is as paramount as knowing the anatomy of an elephant. Hitting the brain of the Ankylosaurus is the best bet for an instant kill; the heart/lung shot requires deep penetration and may subject the hunter to the wrath of a mortally wounded animal, still fully capable of ending your life.

Undoubtedly, you'll need a heavy bore and a good, solid (nonexpanding) bullet, to both penetrate the thick skin of an Ankylosaurus and to provide the necessary tissue damage for a clean kill. The brain shot is the best bet, and that's a

The Perfect Shot for Dinosaurs

double rifle in .450/400 3-inch Nitro Express—like the *eym Model 89B—is a handy and well-balanced choice* *r the Ankylosaurus.*

When loaded with premium bullets like the Woodleigh Hydrostatically Stabilized Solids, the .375 H&H Magnum will serve dinosaur hunter well.

rather small target, so you'll also need a rifle with decent accuracy; horsepower is one thing, but you must hit that brain in order to anchor the beast.

ARMOR-PIERCING RIFLES FOR THE ANKYLOSAURUS

For a beast that is 5½ feet tall, 35 feet long, and 7½ tons, look for cartridges with the best reputation for penetration that have a minimum of 300-grain bullets and a sectional density figure of at least .300. The .375 H&H Belted Magnum, the .416 Rigby and Remington, the .458 Winchester Magnum, and .458 Lott are great choices for bolt-action rifles. For the double-rifle shooter—and there is good cause to have two quick shots—the .450/400, 3-inch NE is a good minimum, and there is nothing wrong with choosing the .470 NE and .500 NE, as the heavy bullets will definitely get the job done.

Traditional safari sights or a low-power scope– 4X–5X at maximum and preferable in detachable mounts—is the way to go. If you work the wind right, a hunter can get relatively close to an Ankylosaur, but not too close: Many who try to get within 15 yards don't live to tell the tale. Make sure you are proficient with your big-bore rifle, consistently hitting a baseball-size area at the 50-yard mark.

The Perfect Shot for Dinosaurs

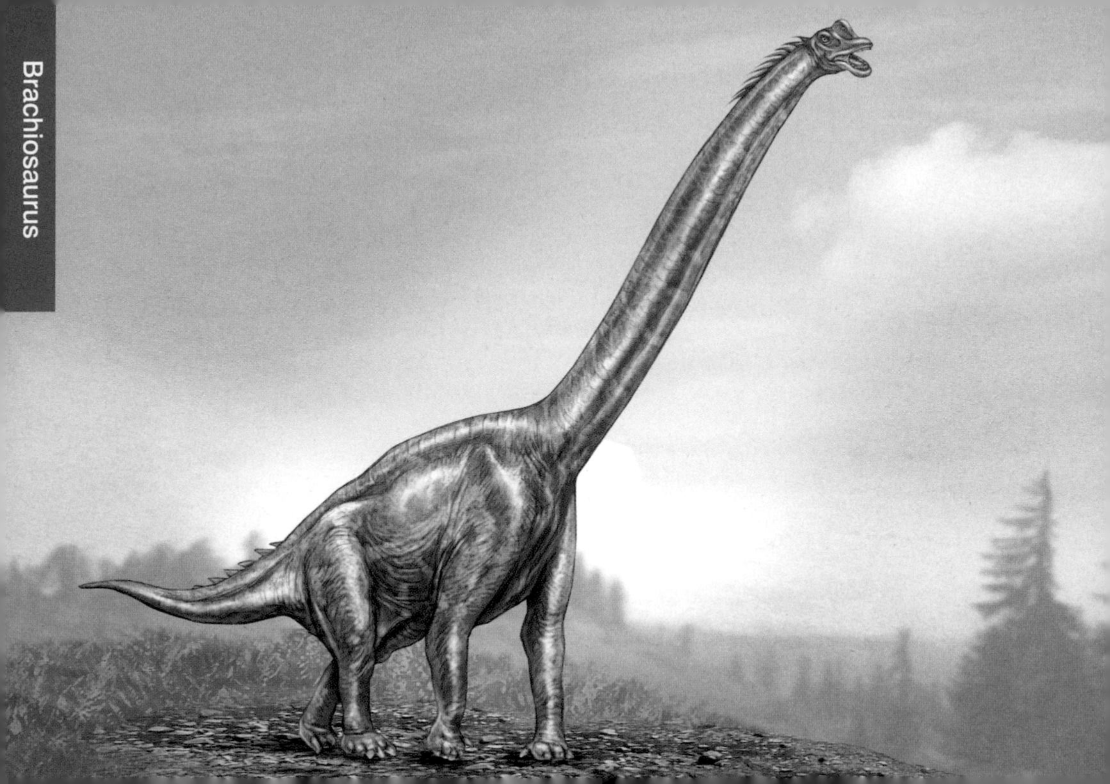

BRACHIOSAURUS—A BRAIN SHOT FROM THE NOSEBLEED SEATS
CHAPTER 12

Are you the kind of hunter who likes to tackle the greatest challenges? Do you enjoy eating that which you've worked so hard to obtain? I can't think of anything that represents the answer to those two questions more than a Brachiosaurus. Yup, I'm talking about Flintstone-level meat festivals, requiring a semitruck to transport your kill and a commercial walk-in freezer to house it.

A true Brachiosaurus is almost twice the size of his more popular cousin—the Brontosaurus—and makes for incredible sport, in spite of Fred's preference for dining upon the latter. Measuring over eighty-five jaw-dropping feet in length and weighing somewhere in the ballpark of eighty tons—how would you even weigh such a beast?—the Brachiosaurus's fifty-foot height allows it to feed on vegetation equally high.

Yes, the meat is on the tough side, but when you've got almost forty tons of it, well, you can see the value in that. They are vegetarians, browsers on an unimaginable level, and the few herds that remain are easily identified by their feeding habits alone. Entire limbs of trees are broken off to feed that inefficient digestive system and, whoa, can a herd of Brachiosaurs leave some droppings on the forest floor!

THE HUNT

The hunting of a Brachiosaurus is one of the few, true, once-in-a-lifetime experiences. Firstly, it will require a team of people upon whom you must absolutely trust your life. This will require a level of dedication

The Perfect Shot for Dinosaurs

that few possess, but if you're lucky enough to have friends of that caliber, you can commence. Secondly, irrespective of which of the team members actually takes the Brachiosaurus, it is a trophy for all involved, as the opportunity to be a part of the exercise is an honor.

Once you've assembled your team, you'll need to plan an ambush, to be coordinated on a military level. Locating the herd—which is, invariably, the hardest part of the endeavor—will require weeks, if not months, of work. Look to those secluded valleys that dot the eastern foothills of the Rocky Mountains for the best chances here in the Americas. In Africa, look to the milder lowlands of Morocco and Tunisia, where there are a few remnant herds that were cut off when the Sahara expanded across northern Africa.

Once you've located the herd, set your men up in order to have a good look at the animals, from as high a vantage point as possible. Then you can take a shot in relative safety, providing you've set up a field of fire in a safe manner, and the shooters are both patient and can exhibit self-control.

SHOT PLACEMENT

Taking a Brachiosaurus is not a difficult ordeal, providing you've thought things through. You'll want to hit the brain—that is the only possible "off" switch on a creature this large—and you'll want to take the shot from a reasonable distance. Safety dictates that you should have at least 150 yards of separation from the animal, as a Brachiosaurus in its death throes can knock down trees three feet in diameter. If you're in the proximity, either the falling trees or the animal itself can easily crush a man. Once the animal

The Perfect Shot for Dinosaurs

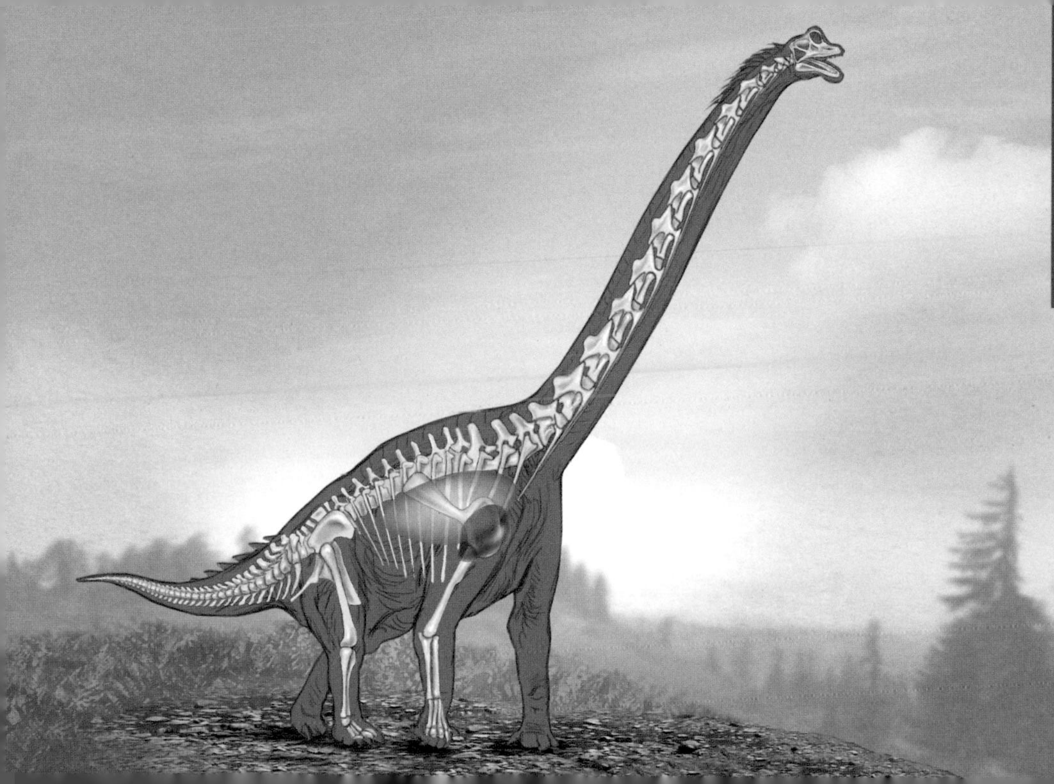

.338 W.IN MAG

ZEISS

The versatile .338 Winchester Magnum makes a good choice for sniping a Brachiosaurus.

has stopped moving, insurance shots in the spine and or heart/lung area with a heavy rifle will ensure that it stays down. This brings us to the choice of weaponry.

GUNS AND LOADS FOR THE BRACHIOSAURUS

The team will need two types of rifles, vastly different from one another. For the brain shots, a sniper-style rifle—set up with a rock-solid scope of at least 12X magnification—will be required. The rifle should be seriously accurate and capable of driving a full-metal-jacket bullet of at least 220 grains at a respectable muzzle velocity.

I would recommend the .300 Winchester Magnum or .300 Norma Magnum as a minimum, and only when loaded with the aforementioned 220-grain pills. Using a .338 Lapua or .338 Norma Magnum with 300-grain FMJs is a better choice.

The .338 Lapua Magnum has the accuracy and horsepower for brain shots on a Brachiosaur.

The Perfect Shot for Dinosaurs

Weatherby
ULTRA-VELOCITY
AMMUNITION

WEATHERBY MAGNUM

20   20

The .460 Weatherby Magnum is one of the most powerful cartridges on earth and makes a perfect choice for secondary body shots on the Brachiosaurus.

The backup gun needs to be a true heavyweight, at a minimum of .500 caliber, carried by the team members who have been designated to fire the insurance shots. The .500 Jeffery, .505 Gibbs Magnum, and .585 Nyati are all good choices for bolt-action rifles, while the .500 NE, .577 NE, and .600 NE are good double-rifle choices. The key here is balance of penetration and wound-channel diameter. You have to penetrate an awful lot of dinosaur to reach the vitals with the backup shots—obviously only the solid, nonexpanding projectiles should be used—and you also want to destroy as much vital tissue as possible.

Have the snipers keep their crosshairs on the animal's brain and/or spine after the first shots are fired. This will give cover to the second team with the heavy-bore rifles. Should that animal so much as twitch, additional brain shots should be taken. If the heavy riflemen approach while the Brachiosaurus is flailing about, you could have a tragedy.

Once the animal is dead and the photos taken, the true work begins. Chainsaws for butchering are a welcome addition to your gear list, and, well, I hope you all like the taste of Brachiosaurus for years to come. . . .

The Perfect Shot for Dinosaurs

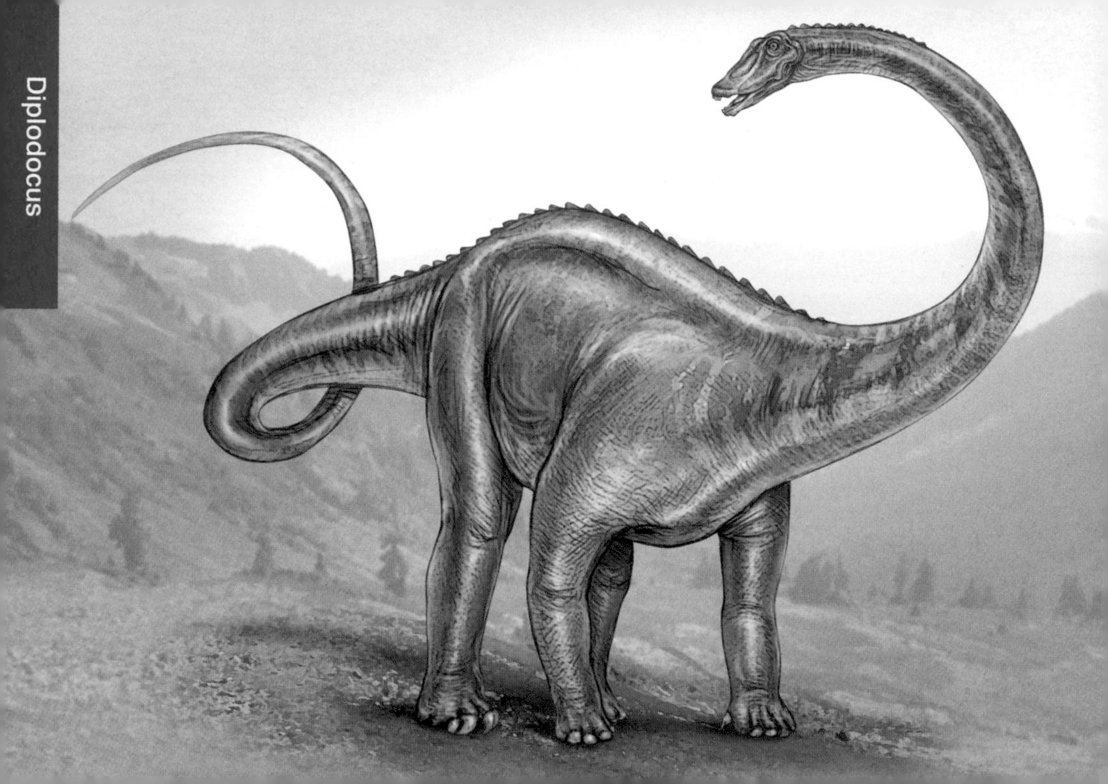

DIPLODOCUS—TREE-TOP DINING
CHAPTER 13

The giant sauropods—while completely docile in their demeanor—can represent one of the greatest challenges to any serious dinosaur hunter. Are they as terrifying as a Tyrannosaur? No, they're not. Are they as crafty as a Velociraptor? Not even close. But, they represent one of the largest chunks of flesh on four feet, and just getting in range makes for a true challenge. With the Diplodocus, we're talking about a beast nearly one hundred feet long, weighs over eighteen tons, and reaches a height of over sixteen feet. They make a fantastic trophy if you have the room to showcase it, but the pursuit of a Diplodocus is no lightweight endeavor. In fact, it may represent one of the greatest labors of your hunting career.

I happen to be a personal friend of Mr. Ralph Steinherr—the famous dinosaur hunting outfitter of Hucky & Steinherr, Pty Ltd. I know for a fact that he has completed the Big Twelve, and he ranks the Diplodocus as one of the most difficult trophies to procure.

"With the head always moving, shot placement is extremely difficult," Steinherr related, "and Hucky and I once had to spend two days perched in a lodgepole pine just to avoid being crushed."

He's one of the most experienced dinosaur hunters I know, so when he said, "They're not hard to kill, but if you're in the wrong position, you'll end up flatter than yesterday's vodka tonic." I for one tend always to heed his advice.

WHERE TO FIND THEM

The greatest concentrations of Diplodocus haunt the desolate forests of the foothills of the Rocky Mountains in Colorado and Wyoming, though the pine forests of Poland has some rare, yet high-quality trophies as well. An infrequent encounter may be had in those remote parts of Turkey where the big wild boars are pursued, and I've seen a couple of decent heads come out of southern Kamchatka.

Contact Steinherr, pay his fee, and let him save you time and frustration.

SHOT PLACEMENT

The Diplodocus is a behemoth of a vegetarian, with a body of incomprehensible proportions. The brain, about the size of grapefruit, is the shot that makes the most sense. Physics being physics, it would take a Stinger missile to knock a Diplodocus over, so the brain is your only option for a quick kill. Look to place that bullet at the crease where the forehead begins to rise vertically.

I suggest that you pass on what may seem like an easy heart shot; though the beast may die, it can easy take you to the afterlife with it as the head and tail flail continuously in the death throes.

Steinherr's comment about getting high up in a tree is not without merit, for a high vantage point can afford a close shot while the Diplodocus feeds on branches and leafy material. It'll take patience, courage, and ice-water in your veins, but if you can remain steady as a herd of huge sauropods feeds past your makeshift vantage point, you may end up as one of the few successful Diplodocus hunters.

You must hit the Diplodocus's brain, and the .338 Winchester Magnum offers a great blend of accuracy and horsepower.

GUNS AND LOADS FOR THE DIPLODOCUS

You'll want a good medium-bore, bolt-action rifle loaded with a premium bullet of decent sectional density. Cartridges like the .338-'06 A-Square, .338 Winchester Magnum, .340 Weatherby, .338 Remington Ultra Magnum, .358 Norma Magnum, and .370 Sako Magnum all possess that blend of bullet weight and speed that will switch a Diplodocus "off." Better still are the faster .375s, like the .375 H&H Magnum and the .378 Weatherby. Shock is appreciable when it comes to the brain shot, yet you'll need a particular degree

The .378 Weatherby Magnum is a fast, hard-hitting choice for braining a Diplodocus.

of accuracy from your rifle. Like a crocodile or hippopotamus in the water, you absolutely need to hit the brain or you'll risk a lost trophy.

Look to bonded core and monometal bullets of between 250 and 300 grains, depending on caliber. The Swift A-Frame, Peregrine Bushmaster, Norma Oryx, Barnes TSX, and Woodleigh Weldcore will all give satisfactory performance on the brain pan of a Diplodocus. Your bullet will quickly create hydrostatic shock in the cranium and debilitate the sauropod. Revel in the moment, for once a Diplodocus is down, the true work begins.

Maiasaura

MAIASAURA—MOMMY DEAREST
CHAPTER 14

If you hunt in the wilds of western Montana—those inhospitable lands that require a long trek with your goods on your back—you may have seen the large, round depressions in the earth dotted with eggshell fragments. If you're lucky, you may have seen the giant tracks of that which made the nesting site, and if you're truly lucky, you may have caught a glimpse of the beast itself. The Maiasaura is one of the duck-billed dinosaurs, an herbivore who is no more aggressive than it is comely. However, they make for excellent sport for the dinosaur hunter.

The Maiasaura is a herd animal, and that is one of the attributes that makes it so difficult to hunt, for to get that "perfect trophy," you'll need to fool the many sets of eyes and nostrils that are always on high alert. A hunt for a Maiasaura will remind you of selecting the best *dagga* boy from a Cape buffalo herd. You must be wary, you must be cunning, and you must ultimately be a hunter at the top of his/her game.

The trophy here is not horn, spike, or tooth size; it's the taking of an old bull Maiasaura from the herd. The old ones tend to stay to the rear—as is common in most herd situations—in order to guard the females and young from predatory attack. You can easily judge a trophy Maiasaura bull from the shape of his head and bill; the female's bill remains longer and sharper while a trophy male's bill will be more broad and worn. There is also a difference in size between the genders: The females tend to measure about twenty-five feet long,

Maiasaura

and a trophy bull will be at least five feet longer. Moreover, the muscles on the neck of a bull are more clearly pronounced, and, overall, the neck just "looks" definitely stronger.

The Maiasaura has the ability to walk as both a quadruped—predominately while grazing—as well as biped, the latter normally reserved for times of duress, when food is only available at greater heights, or when the dinosaur is alarmed, as in the presence of a predator.

THE HUNT

Pursuing a herd of Maiasaura requires incredible physical stamina. You'll need to travel light, taking with you only the absolute necessities, and you'll need to rely on your skills as a woodsman for survival. Tracking is a viable method of obtaining a trophy Maiasaura, or glassing will also work if the hunter can find a high vantage point. After that, it's all about an appropriate stalk. Either way—tracking or glassing—you'll need to get close. Anything over a hundred yards is considered a very long shot on a Maiasaura because you'll need not only accurate shooting but also the greatest amount of kinetic energy possible in order to secure an animal of this magnitude.

Once the shot is taken, it is not uncommon for many members of the herd to gather around the wounded creature (especially if you've taken the dominant herd bull) and form a defense. It's at this time you'll need to be patient and wait for the wounded beast to succumb. Do not try to drive off the herd. There have been many reported instances where a hunter or hunters have been trampled to death while attempting to turn the rest of the herd.

Maiasaura

The Perfect Shot for Dinosaurs

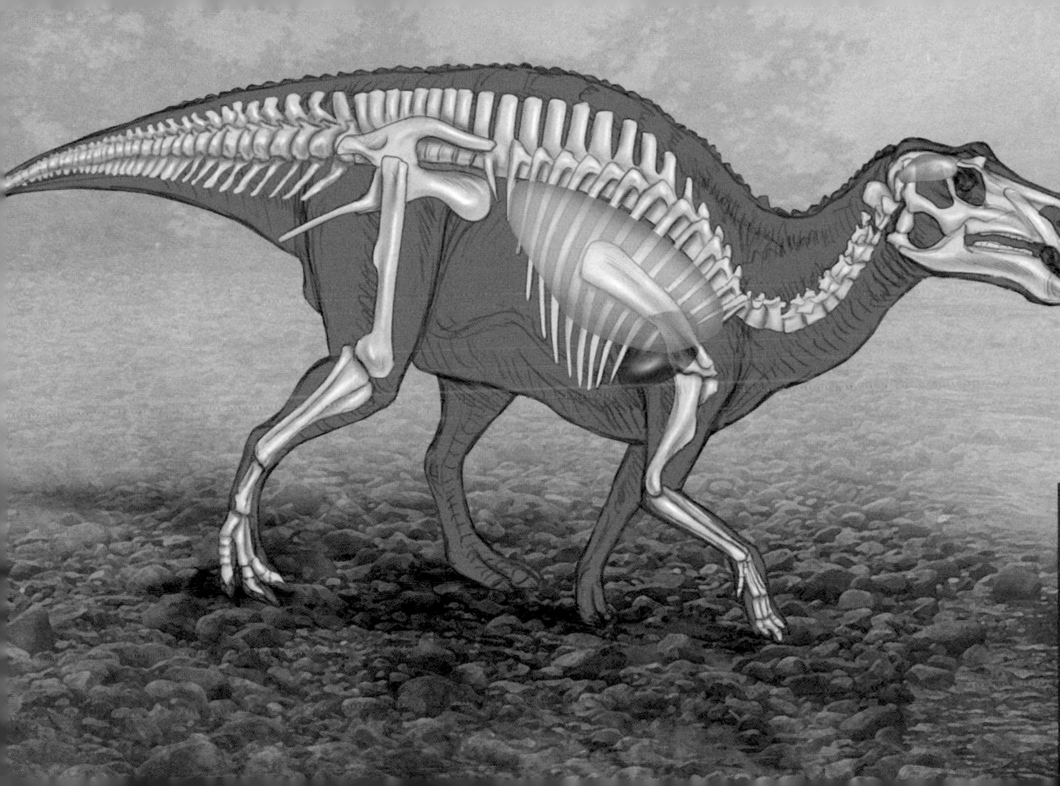

Maiasaura

The .450 Rigby is a modern update of the .450 Nitro Express formula, giving the former a 200 fps velocity boost; it's perfect for the Maiasaura.

The Perfect Shot for Dinosaurs

SHOT PLACEMENT

Taking a shot at a Maiasaura when it's standing on its rear legs is much preferred to shooting the beast when it is on all fours. In the standing position, the animal's balance is diminished, and his reaction time will be slowed. In that upright position, the forelimbs will seem to hang limply, thus allowing a better angle for you to place the shot in the heart/ lung area. It also usually allows for a clear, stable shot at the brain.

GUNS AND LOADS FOR THE MAIASAURA

With a steep shoulder and driving bullets of up to 550 grains, the .450 Rigby is a great choice for hunting the Maiasaura.

The sheer size of a Maiasaura requires a bullet of appreciable diameter and of stout construction, yet the rifle must be both pleasant to carry and equally durable. They stand over eight feet tall, are thirty feet long, and weigh over ten tons. I personally prefer cartridges in the lower .40s, like the .416 Remington, .416 Rigby, and .404 Jeffery, and my choice in a rifle is for a synthetic stock with a light, low-power scope.

My own favorite for these types of situations is a Legendary Arms Works Big Five rifle that has been hot-rodded by custom gunmaker Mark Bansner. The rifle features a hand-laid fiberglass stock, and all the exposed metal has been properly coated with Cerakote. Using the Norma African PH factory loads, it'll drive a Woodleigh 450-grain solid at 2,165 fps, and the increased bullet weight (the .404 loads normally top out at 400 grains) and sectional density makes a big difference in the field.

If you can find a rifle of similar weight and durability chambered in a .458 Lott or .450 Rigby, the 500- and 550-grain solids are even better, though the recoil will definitely ramp up. A trim .500 Jeffery, driving a 570-grain bullet at 2,300 fps is even more effective, though at a weight that is easy to carry, you'll find that the recoil can be terrible. However, a cartridge the likes of the .500 Jeffery will sort out the largest of beasts and engender all sorts of confidence.

(Left) Peregrine Bushmaster bullets loaded in the .404 Jeffery will give fantastic penetration, even through tough dinosaur hide.

Ornithomimus

ORNITHOMIMUS—THE OSTRICH OF THE COLD CLIMES
CHAPTER 15

If you've been fortunate enough to spend any amount of time on safari on the Dark Continent, you're familiar with the mannerisms of the African ostrich. This goofy-looking flightless bird, so often depicted with its head in the sand, is actually a worthy foe. The ostrich has adapted to the hot climate of Southern Africa, and considering the level of predation that the African continent has to offer, it is truly a success story. The ostrich has been equipped with both the tools necessary to fend off the predators and as well as the physiognomy to survive in the harsh climate. While the world believes that its nearest relative may be the Australian emu, few are aware of the ostrich's older relative, that great-great-great granduncle of the southern Canadian province of Alberta—the Ornithomimus.

Ornithomimus means "bird mimic," and while it looks like the predecessor of the modern-day bird, it is most certainly incapable of flight. This theropod is both rare and secretive. It is larger than its avian relations, yet equally attuned to its environment. It is an omnivore, a scavenger, and an opportunist. The fine feathers that cover its torso, neck, and the stunted appendages—where wings should be—transition into scaly, bare skin on the legs. If ever a turkey hunter were looking for a challenge, the Ornithomimus is it. The bird mimic can be taller than seven feet when standing erect and measure over twelve feet long when lurching forward on the run. It has highly developed vision—those oversize eye sockets will pick up the slightest movement within 200 yards. A mature Ornithomimus represents a true trophy to any collector of the major bird species and their relations.

Ornithomimus

WHERE TO FIND THEM

What can't the .30-'06 Springfield handle? That list includes the Ornithomimus, for certain.

The forests of southern Alberta are the best place to find a trophy Ornithomimus, as the habitat is perfect: rugged, isolated, and thick with vegetation. You'll have to dedicate yourself to the task, however, as the spring mating grounds are not easy to find, and stringent scouting methods are what seem to produce the most reliable results. Follow the watercourses, and look for huge, three-toe tracks that resemble the turkey's—at five times the size! Even on rocky ground, Ornithomimus tracks will be evident as the four-inch-long claw will leave a distinct scrape on the larger rocks and stones. Droppings along the shore are another indication of the presence of a 'Mimus—as experienced hunters call them. Look for the large, milky-white droppings in elongated clusters.

SHOT PLACEMENT

The Ornithomimus is not huge, averaging about twelve feet in length, standing nine feet tall, and tipping the scale at four hundred pounds. Aim for the base of the skull in order to break the neck, and this will result in

The Perfect Shot for Dinosaurs

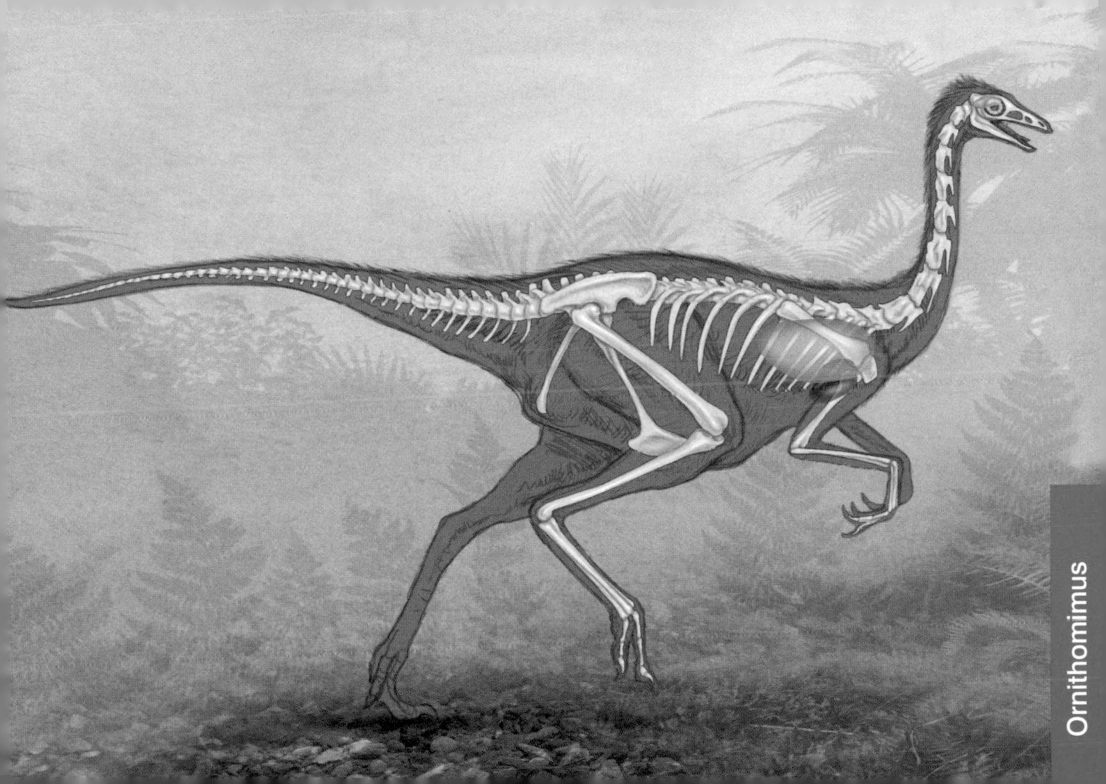
Ornithomimus

The author glassing for the herd of Ornithomimosaurs.

Ornithomimus

a quick kill. If you have a large family over for Thanksgiving dinner, a roast Ornithomimus will fill many bellies.

GUNS FOR THE ORNITHOMIMUS

An Ornithomimus can be taken with stout loads of buckshot from a large shotgun, or with any medium-caliber rifle. Its chosen terrain is usually wooded, so it will be necessary to keep shots on the close side. For really close-up shots, I recommend using a shotgun. If a rifle is more your style, my preference is for a classic cartridge like

The classic .308 Winchester makes an excellent choice for the Ornithomimus.

the 7x57 Mauser, .308 Winchester, and .30-'06 Springfield. The heavier calibers, at a moderate velocity—the .338-'06 A-Square, .318 Westley Richards, .35 Whelen, and 9.3x62 Mauser—will also make a good choice.

The Ornithomimus can certainly cover the ground quickly, so I prefer a good low-power scope, with the classic Leupold 1.5–5X20 making a sound choice. You can place shots accurately out to 200 yards or more, but the low settings offer a nice, wide field of view for the running shots. Place a premium bullet, like the Nosler Partition, Swift A-Frame, Barnes TSX, or Woodleigh Weldcore with a decent sectional density, in the center of the body, and the Ornithomimus will be yours.

Ornithomimus

PACHYCEPHALOSAURUS—THE HEAD BUTT THAT WALKS
CHAPTER 16

Deep in the Wyoming highlands, in an area surrounding the town of Cody, lives a rare and unique dinosaur named Pachycephalosaurus. It is not a large dinosaur, and it is rather comical-looking in its appearance. With a scaly tonsure that ascends to a dome, it looks like an angry monk with an over-developed sense of bravado. The word Pachycephalosaurus literally means "thick-headed lizard," and one view of the overdeveloped cranium explains our name for this creature.

Make no mistake: The Pachycephalosaurus is a dinosaur that can turn the tables on a hunter very quickly, for it is quick and fearless. At six feet tall, sixteen feet long, and weighing nearly one thousand pounds, Ol' Pachy is ready for a fight. Having survived through the eons, he is the banty rooster of the dinosaur populations. Like the mighty Jack Russell terrier, he does not realize how small it is, and he has no problem taking on enemies much larger than himself. I've actually seen one giggle at a specimen of *Homo sapiens*.

If you've been in those hills—the Big Horn Mountains and the surrounding plateau—you may have heard the thunderous crashes so commonly attributed to the mating rituals of the Rocky Mountain bighorn sheep. Not all those sounds are sheep; in fact, many echo the collision of two dominant male Pachycephalosauruses in combat for mating rights.

The "bald" cranial developments of the Pachycephalosaur, along with the ring of stunted hornlike growths around the base of the skull, are the signature of this species. Standing a bit more than three feet when walking, the Pachycephalosaurus will measure more than fifteen feet from nose to tail. In extreme cases, big males can weigh up to nine hundred and fifty pounds,

It is his low center of gravity that makes the herbivore so dangerous, for in a blink of an eye, it can turn on its pursuer and deliver a knockout head butt. It's imperative for the hunter to understand that the Pachycephalosaur becomes aggressive during the mating season, much like a bull elephant in musth. My suggestion is that you exercise extreme caution with any encounter closer than twenty paces.

THE HUNT

Pursuing a Pachycephalosaur into the Wyoming mountains is a beautiful hunt, yet the success rate is low, at best. Attain the high ground and glass down into the small openings in the forest for the movements of the Pachycephalosaur. Sunny days are best for hunting this dinosaur as the sun will easily reflect off its bald head. If that technique doesn't work for you, look for tracks along the numerous watercourses in broken country: The three-toe rear foot will be offset by a telltale five-toe front foot, especially when it's feeding. You will need to use your best hunting skills to get the drop on a Pachycephalosaur.

The best trophies are the larger animals with their thick, worn, cranial horns. Like old *dagga* boys, they won't score as high as the younger males, but they represent the old warriors, the veterans. These are the guys past their prime breeding stage, so a trophy from this age group will help maintain the integrity of the gene pool.

Speaking of the scoring system for dinosaurs, I'm not a fan. In the last century, there was a minor revolution to eliminate the preference for taking young Cape buffaloes with their larger, more pointed

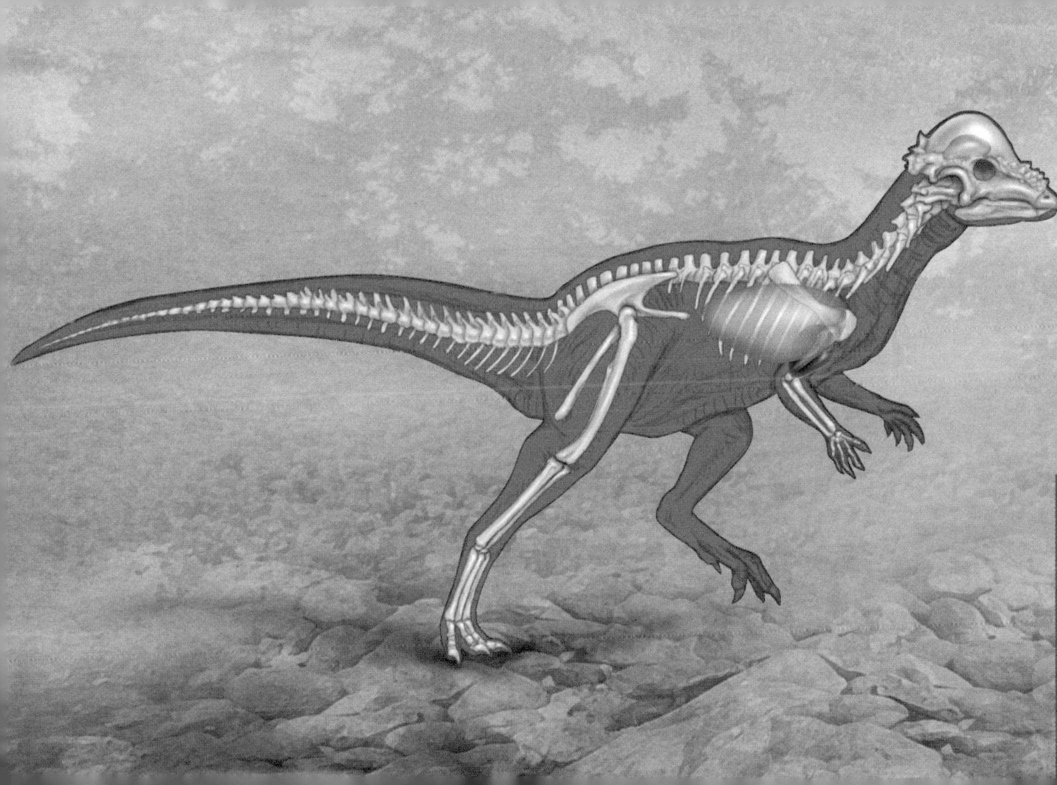

Pachycephalosaurus

Massaro zeroing his Pachycephalosaur rifle—a Winchester Model 70 Super Express in the classic .375 H&H Magnum.

Pachycephalosaurus

Pachycephalosaurus

Pachycephalosaurus

For double rifles, the .375 flanged makes an excellent choice for hunting the Pachycephalosaur.

horns . . . but soft bosses. We succeeded in that battle; now we need to do the same thing for the scoring systems for the various dinosaurs.

SHOT PLACEMENT

Go for a body shot on the Pachycephalosaur. Place the shot a hand's width behind the stunted forelimbs, one-third up the body, and the heart/lung area will be destroyed. Upon follow-up, place one good shot into the prominent, raised spine, either at the highest spot above the hips, or at the junction of the neck and body. These and these alone will prevent the Pachycephalosaurus from making dust of your skull with its devastating head butt.

RIFLES FOR THE PACHYCEPHALOSAURUS

The best choices for a body shot include those cartridges using a bullet of 200 to 300 grains at a moderate velocity of, say, no more than 2,500 fps. Additionally, I much prefer the semispitzer and round-nose and flat-nose bullets like the Swift A-Frame, Woodleigh Weldcore, Peregrine Bushmaster, and North Fork semispitzer. Look to the old .318 Westley Richards, .338-06 A-Square, .35 Whelen, 9.3x62 Mauser, and .375 H&H Magnum.

I have one final note worth mentioning: The underbelly of the Pachycephalosaurus makes excellent leather for boots, cartridge belts, and gun slips. Save that hide for future use unless you're doing a full-body mount.

Pachycephalosaurus

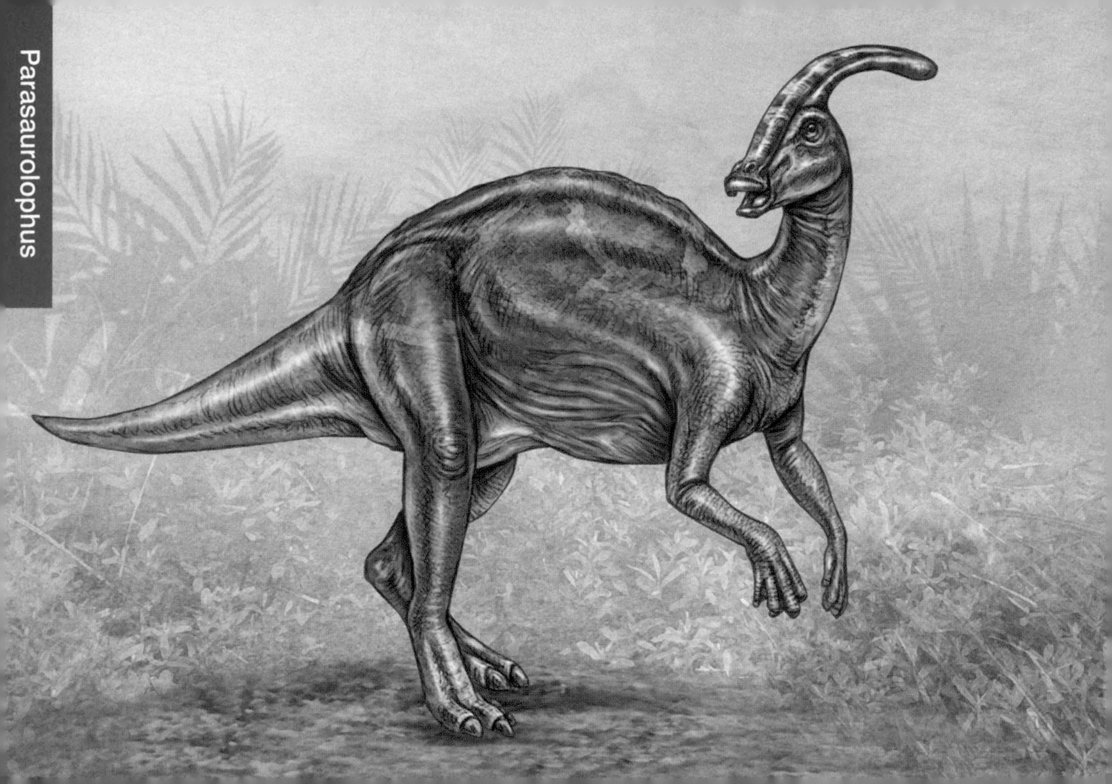

Parasaurolophus

PARASAUROLOPHUS—THE TRUMPETER
CHAPTER 17

In the forested areas of northern New Mexico near the Colorado border hides a holdover from the Cretaceous Period—the Parasaurolophus. This same area where elk hunting is so fantastic lives this brute of a herbivore, capable of both bipedal and quadrupedal movement. The Parasaurolophus has an unmistakable cranial crest that serves a multitude of purposes—including proper thermoregulation—but is used primarily for its unforgettable call.

That call . . . is horrid! It's a combination of the death bellow of a bear and a student of the French horn practicing on his brand-new instrument. It has been incorrectly attributed to a variety of species, including the mythical Sasquatch, and as a point of note, the Sasquatch call is so firmly rooted in the local mythos that the village of Jemez Springs actually holds a festival in its honor. How awkward would they feel knowing it is actually the Parasaurolophus call they are celebrating?

The area in northern New Mexico that the Parasaurolophus inhabits is a rugged place, predominately timbered, yet remote enough that a remnant population of these ancient beasts thrives to this day. I have heard the call but have yet to have a trophy-quality Parasaurolophus within my sights, a condition I am working hard to remedy. Yes, I'll happily take a bull elk when I get to return to an area like the Jicarilla, but make no mistake—that will not be my priority.

There is no misidentifying a Parasaurolophus when you see your first one: They are twelve feet tall when on all fours and over sixteen feet when standing erect, as they will flight. At a length of over thirty feet, I refuse to believe you'll be anything but astonished when you realize how little noise this dinosaur makes for its size. Its scaled skin is colored to blend in perfectly with a coniferous forest, and its size makes it easily overlooked should it remain motionless in the forest.

THE HUNT

Hunting a Parasaurolophus will require time; any hurried affair will result in frustration. For those who do not live near that region—including this author—it can very easily become a quest, but if you put your time in, you'll very likely find the spoor you're after. Look for the huge, three-toe rear tracks, and the correlatively tiny front tracks. You'll also see neatly cropped vegetation to a height of three or four feet in areas of over an acre; the digestive system of the Parasaurolophus is not exactly what you'd call efficient.

Once spoor is located, it becomes a game of stamina. Are your legs up to the challenge? Can you successfully track an animal with a ten-foot stride in time to get the shot? That is up to you, dear hunter.

There are those who have modified the tubular elk-bugle calls to reproduce the low, resonating tones of the Parasaurolophus, though I suggest you obtain an accurate sound file so as to properly replicate the tones without clearing the forest of life.

The Perfect Shot for Dinosaurs

The .416 Remington Magnum—giving identical ballistics to the .416 Rigby—is a smart choice for general dinosaur hunting.

The Perfect Shot for Dinosaurs

SHOT PLACEMENT

The skull of a Parasaurolophus—minus the long crest—can exceed two feet in length, and the small brain lies just behind the eye sockets. From the side, the brain lies at the rear of the orbital socket—easy to pick out—but frontally things can get more difficult. The large nostrils and sloping skull can make for difficult target acquisition, as the location of the brain will change in relation to the frontal part of the head. Watch the eyes, and try to keep your shot no more than an inch up or down of the line between the eyes, depending on how the head is tilted.

The venerable .404 Jeffery makes an excellent Parasaurolophus cartridge, especially when loaded with modern bullets like the Woodleigh Hydro Solid.

RIFLES FOR THE PARASAUROLOPHUS

Without question, the sheer size of the Parasaurolophus requires a stout bullet, of appropriate bore diameter. A bolt-action rifle makes the most sense, considering the distances you'll need to pack

The Perfect Shot for Dinosaurs

Here you have an American Hunting Rifle in .416 Rigby. Based on the CZ550 action, this combination makes for an excellent Parasaurolophus rig.

The Perfect Shot for Dinosaurs

in. I feel the .338 bores—and only when driving the heavy 250-grain solids—are an absolute minimum for the serious Parasaurolophus hunter. Better choices are the .375 H&H, .404 Jeffery, and the .416 Rigby, Remington, and Ruger; all possess the high-sectional density, nonexpanding bullets that will effectively reach the vitals of a Parasaurolophus, and all are capable of the pinpoint accuracy required to make a brain shot, should that be warranted. You'll want a good, low-power scope—preferably with an illuminated reticle for those thick conifer forests—that will allow a wide field of view.

As an aside, the hide of a Parasaurolophus can be mesmerizing at higher magnifications—it looks much like an elephant hide.

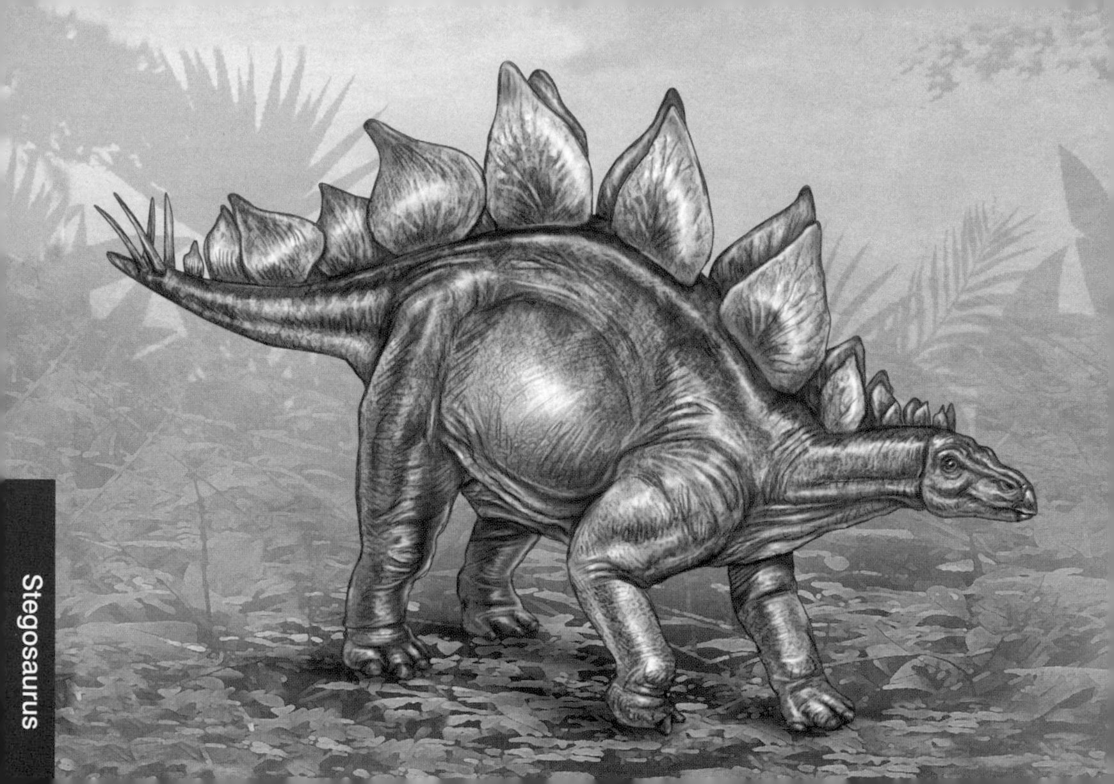

Stegosaurus

STEGOSAURUS—THE GREAT THAGOMIZER
CHAPTER 18

Greek for "covered lizard," a Stegosaurus has bony, spiked plates on its back and tail, and it is from these tail spikes that the term "thagomizer" is derived. It has short forelimbs, longer rear limbs, and that classic row of moveable pointed plates rising from the spine and going all the way down the tail. A stegosaur is roughly the size of a large African elephant bull, standing nine feet tall, weighing nearly three and a half tons, and measuring nearly thirty feet long, nose to tail. It is easily identifiable by its silhouette alone.

The first skeletons, and live specimens, were found concentrated in southwestern Wyoming. The largest subspecies—*Stegosaurus ungulatus*—can pose a formidable threat, especially if pushed into a confrontation. While all the Stegosaurs are herbivores, they are properly equipped to settle the score with any and all predators, including hunters. Those plates along the back are attached via flexible muscles and tendons, and can be directed to ward off attacks from above. The spiked tail seems to move with a mind of its own, which isn't far off the mark.

THE HUNT

You'll want to use the wind, as the stegosaurus prefers to feed into the wind, and approach the beast from the rear. I'd also recommend practicing your marksmanship, as eons of super-predators have forced

Stegosaurus

the stegosaur to evolve into a wary creature, whose first instinct is to thrash with the spiked tail and ask questions later—that's the reason it's called the "thagomizer." The stegosaur hunter's mantra—and believe me it's well-founded—is "Not too close, yet not too far."

SHOT PLACEMENT

You see, all Stegosaurs have a small brain located in the skull, but they also have a secondary brain located between their hips. We hunters can, and should, take full advantage of that feature. The "front" brain of a stegosaur is very small—roughly the size of a large chicken nugget—and can be difficult to hit unless you are very close. But that rear, secondary brain is much larger, and while it doesn't have all the cognitive power that the primary brain does, a well-placed solid from a Nitro Express rifle can and will debilitate the entire rear section of the animal. That means the highly dangerous spiked tail will be put out of action, allowing you to calmly take the heart/lung shot.

Just like taking a brain shot on an elephant, you'll need to envision the location of the rear brain from any angle, and be sure not to tickle the trigger unless you are certain your shot will find it.

GUNS AND LOADS FOR THE STEGOSAURUS

I prefer Nitro Express cartridges of .450 caliber and up because you may have to penetrate heavy hip bones, and in the bolt guns, there really is no point in a cartridge less than the .416 Rigby and Remington. While penetration is key, horsepower is also warranted, as is frontal diameter. I personally prefer a good double rifle in .470 Nitro Express as the bullets possess a sectional density high enough to smash bone

The Perfect Shot for Dinosaurs

Stegosaurus

Stegosaurus

Massaro drawing a bead on a
Stegosaurus bull.

and still reach the brain. A .470 NE double will generate 5,000 ft.-lbs. of muzzle energy, which can break a hip bone, and it will allow for a quick follow-up shot.

If you prefer a bolt-action rifle, the .458 Lott and .450 Rigby are about ideal, with the .505 Gibbs and .500 Jeffery giving an added sense of security, should the Stegosaur turn and charge. Monometal solids—capable of the famous straight line penetration we've all come to appreciate—are the only way to go; the thick hide and heavy bones will make a mockery of any softpoint on the market.

Massaro practicing with a .458 Lott, a good choice for the Stegosaurus.

Due to the sheer size of a Stegosaur and the thick vegetation in which he is most comfortable, you should forego telescopic in favor of traditional safari express sights or a red-dot sight. Field of view is paramount, as you'll be picking a spot on a large patch of green-gray hide against a green background.

FOLLOW-UP

Do not, under any circumstances, fool about with a wounded Stegosaur. The beak is razor sharp, and the jaws have the strength to literally bite you in half. Proceed with caution, watching the wind and looking

The Perfect Shot for Dinosaurs

Stegosaurus

A good double rifle, chambered in the famous .470 Nitro Express, will certainly anchor the biggest of Stegosaurs.

Stegosaurus

for other herd members who refuse to abandon their friend. Pay the insurance, putting two shots into the heart/lung area when approaching what appears to be a dead Stegosaur: You don't want the business end—the tail—thumping you, and you don't want that beak turning on you.

NOTES

I encountered my first Stegosaur while on a hunt near Elk Mountain, Wyoming. We were calling coyotes and using a live dog for a decoy. When that lovable pooch wandered into a gully, thick with cedars, I gave chase and found what the dog was after. An old Stegosaur, long in the tooth and failing from the harshness of that winter, had lain down for one final time. I spent near an hour just watching and learning. Its herd mates had gathered around it, and I watched the dynamic between all the generations within that herd. That learning experience led me to my first Stegosaur—a barren female who had seen better days.

TROPHY ASSESSMENT

Both male and female Stegosaurus have the famous plates, so both make an acceptable trophy. Like the Cape buffalo, trophy score should not be indicative of what we want in a true trophy animal. Look to the Stegosaurus with worn plates and tail spines; those are the true trophies as they've survived the predators, as well as hunting pressure.

The Perfect Shot for Dinosaurs

Stegosaurus

Styracosaurus

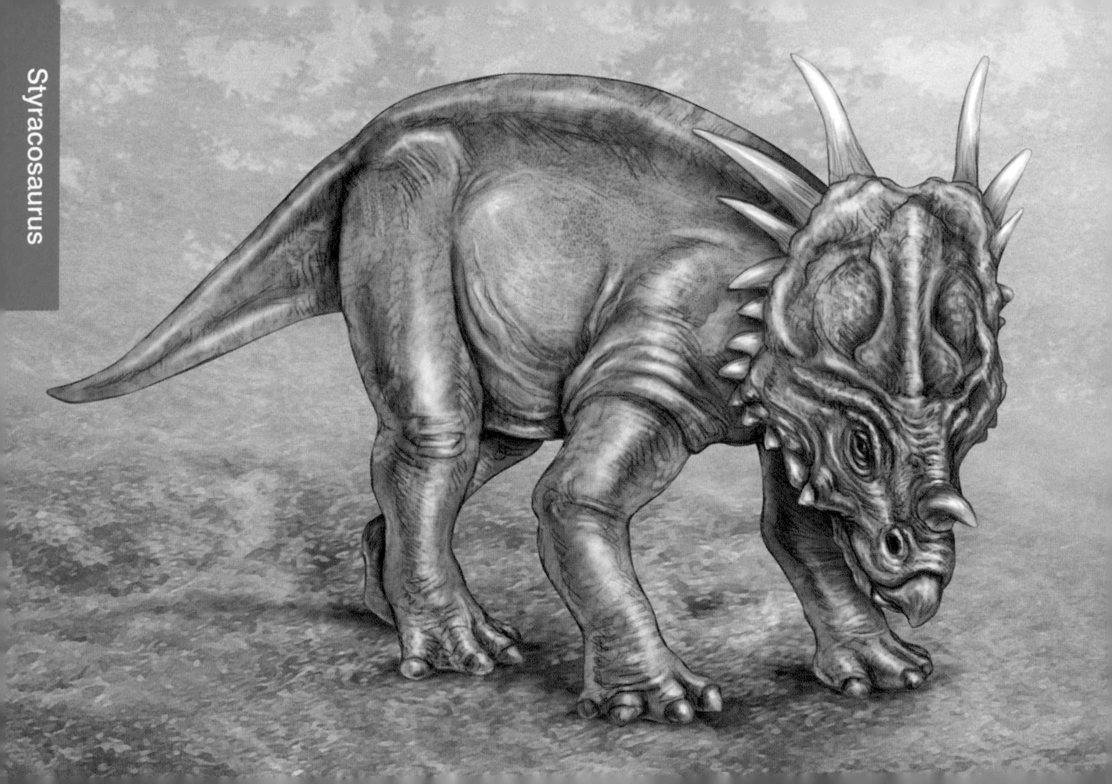

STYRACOSAURUS—A SPEAR-TIPPED POWERHOUSE
CHAPTER 19

While you may be more familiar with its younger cousin, the Triceratops, the Styracosaurus is possibly the more dangerous of the pair. The Styracosaurus is smaller than the Triceratops but ferocious. It is faster and can use its horned frill to terrible effect. They are stout creatures, measuring eighteen to twenty feet in overall length and weighing up to up three tons, though they stand only six feet at the shoulder.

A fully mature Styracosaur makes a fantastic trophy, based on its rarity alone, but look for a trophy Styracosaur to have a horn length of up to twenty-four inches. It is a herd animal, with a sharp, parrotlike beak, a single horn located at the end of the nose, and a low center of gravity. The forelimbs are much shorter than the rear legs, giving the Styracosaurus that jacked-up sports car look, and the thick hide, when combined with the additional horns at the top of the huge frill, will certainly ward off even the largest predators.

Being a herd animal, the Styracosaurus will actually behave in much the same fashion as the Cape buffalo, with the large males remaining at the back of the herd as a sentinel and a protection for all. The best trophy bulls have large, yet worn horns, and will display muted colors on their frills. However, even where there are lots of Styracosauruses, there still aren't many. They are restricted to the most remote portions of the northern Rocky Mountains, preferring to remain hidden in the dense vegetation, where they feed slowly throughout the day. That sharp beak will clip short vegetation off cleanly, and that's a telltale sign of Styracosaurs presence—well, that and the signature three-toe tracks and huge droppings.

THE HUNT

The pursuit of a Styracosaurus is a rugged, painstaking, and lengthy affair. It will require you to trek deep into the wilds—usually carrying all your gear on your back—and to spend an exorbitant amount of time with a good binocular. Once the herd is located—if you're lucky—a stalk will ensue, hoping to catch the big bulls at the rear of the herd. You'll want the best lightweight clothing and rugged, comfortable boots, in addition to the best survival gear kit you can muster. A good GPS, in addition to a satellite phone for emergencies would also be a good idea.

SHOT PLACEMENT

"Beware the frill!" is the mantra of both the Styracosaurus and Triceratops hunters, and with good reason. The brain cavity is about three inches above the line of the eye sockets—when facing head-on—so keep that in mind, as any shot placed higher than that will hit nothing vital.

Your best bet is a heart/lung shot placed when the animal is broadside, and multiple shots wouldn't be a bad idea, either. Most importantly, during the follow-up, put one last shot in the spine from a distance of no closer than ten yards; those spear-tip horns at the top of the frill will bring your dinosaur hunting days to an immediate halt should they connect with your body in an up-close-and-personal way.

The Perfect Shot for Dinosaurs

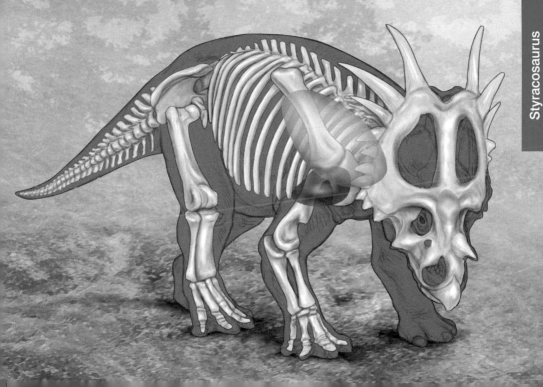

If one were to choose a double rifle for the Styracosaurus, it would be hard to beat the Heym 89B in .450/400 3-inch Nitro Express.

Mark Bansner makes a great all-weather rifle, and this beautiful .404 Jeffery would be just about perfect for the Styracosaurus.

RIFLES FOR THE STYRACOSAURUS

Choosing the right rifle is a bit of a quandary for me because you'll need both plenty of horsepower to make a clean kill, yet a rifle light enough to pack around the wild places. This pretty much takes the double rifles off the menu, leaving a bolt-action rifle as the predominate choice. I'd recommend a rifle with a synthetic stock, with either stainless metal or a good layer of Cerakote to ward off the elements.

The Perfect Shot for Dinosaurs

A trim, light rifle in .375 H&H Magnum makes all the sense in the world for a pack-in hunt for a Styracosaur.

I prefer the .375 H&H Magnum, the .404 Jeffery, or one of the .416s, as they can be housed in a portable rifle, yet when topped with a good solid, have the penetrative qualities necessary to reach the vital organs. Look to the Barnes Banded Solids, the Woodleigh Hydrostatically Stabilized Solid, and the North Fork Cup Solid for the best penetration, for you'll need to break shoulder bones or the thick skull for a quick kill. Top that rifle with a good low-power scope like the Leupold VX-6 in 1–6X24 or the Swarovski V8i in 1–8X24, both good for shots out to 150 yards.

Triceratops

TRICERATOPS—THE THREE-HORNED BEHEMOTH
CHAPTER 20

I was on the phone with a good buddy who had just returned from his hunting block overseas, and he uttered a phrase that caused me to ask him to repeat it. I thought I had heard him correctly, but it didn't make sense. Upon his repetition, I realized that I *had* heard him correctly. What he said to me was that he had actually seen a Triceratops, the most famous of the ceratopsid dinosaurs.

The late Jay T. Carlson was one of the few professional hunters to have operated in the Philippines, and he was my friend. "I was hunting with *(a rather prominent figure in the hunting industry)* for buffalo," Carlson related, "when I saw the same track I'd seen in Montana. Two hours later, we SAW a Triceratops! They're huge! Dammit, they're here too. It was unreal."

The Triceratops is one of the most visually identifiable dinosaurs of them all. Just show a picture of a Triceratops to the average four-year-old, and he or she will more than likely make the correct call. The Triceratops is believed to have gone extinct at the K-Pg [Cretaceous–Paleogene] boundary, but we all know that's not true. It's hard to believe that most still try to push that false "mega-extinction" theory upon us. The Triceratops was one of the dinosaurs that migrated to North America from modern Asia, across the land bridge. Based on Carlson's evidence, however, a dual evolution occurred, much like our moose, elk, and brown bear.

Triceratops literally translates to "three-horn face," with good reason: The two horns above the eyes and the single, prominent horn on the nasal structure makes for a striking image. The large frill that guards the neck is brightly colored and is used as a dominant display among males when looking for a mate. A sharp, parrotlike beak completes the facial structure.

Thirty feet long and standing ten feet tall at the withers, a Triceratops is nothing to fool around with. It can crush a man by accident, and if cornered, will easily rearrange your anatomy, especially if you encounter a brooding female. A large male will tip the scales at thirteen tons—easily twice that of a big elephant bull—and he has the capability to decapitate a hunter with his sharp beak. While the Triceratops are a prey animal for the Tyrannosaurs, little else under the sun possesses the ability to take on a Triceratops, save for an experienced hunter.

WHERE TO FIND THEM

There are several remnant herds scattered throughout southern Asia—according to reports—but the largest population thrives along the edges of what was the inland sea just east of the Rocky Mountains. Eastern Wyoming and Montana as well as southern Alberta are where I'd recommend a hunter begin his/her pursuit for a trophy-quality Triceratops. Look for the tracks—three toes on the front and four toes on the rear foot—in the creekbeds of forested areas; it shouldn't be long before you find spoor, if you get deep enough.

They can also be found in selected regions of Africa. According to a recent YouTube video, Donald Trump Jr. shot a near world-record Rowland Ward Triceratops sometime in the latter part of 2017. Perhaps the video is still available for viewing online. This means, of course, that there are remnant herds throughout the world, but in isolated pockets.

The Perfect Shot for Dinosaurs

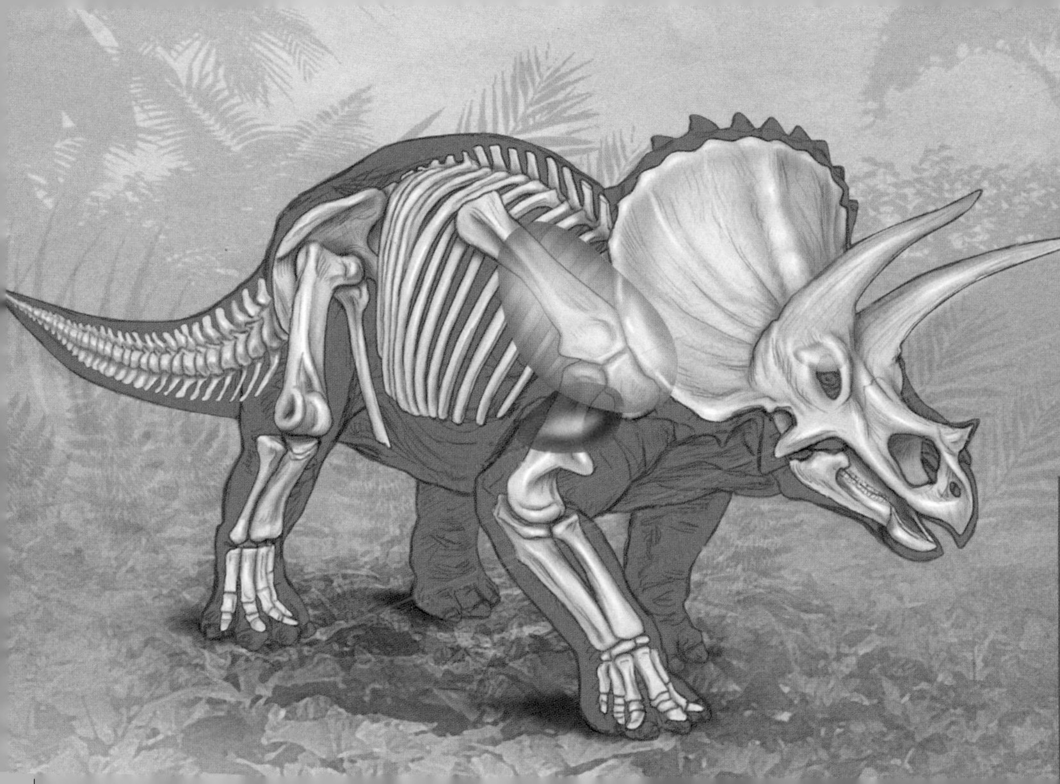

Massaro examining the mud rubbing of a bull Triceratops.

THE HUNT

The pursuit of a Triceratops is primarily a stalking hunt; you'll need to put miles on your boots if you expect any chance of success. The odds are that you'll catch one feeding slowly, and at that point in time things change. That large parrotlike nose can detect faint scents from far away, and if your scent is discovered, you may be in serious trouble. While the Triceratops is a herbivore, it will not hesitate to turn and charge, and more than one hunter has ended up a dino shish kebab when trying to get too close. When you "make contact," gather your thoughts, come up with a plan, and make sure you know your rifle.

SHOT PLACEMENT

Shooting a Triceratops from the rear can be tricky as the large frill seems to cover

The Perfect Shot for Dinosaurs

Triceratops

Rigby's Big Game rifle, chambered in the classic .416 Rigby, is a smart and classy choice for the Triceratops.

The .416 Remington Magnum is relatively easy on the shoulder, yet offers the penetration needed to anchor a Triceratops.

the brain from the rear, so a raking heart/lung shot or a spine shot may be your only option. You'll need a fast-handling rifle—either double or bolt—because a backup shot will invariably be needed. If you're winded and the Triceratops turns to face you, things actually improve.

While the nasal area—replete with its impressive horn—looks impenetrable, there are actually large, hollow passages that will allow you to slip a bullet into the brain. Place your shot directly on the muzzle—as the Triceratops looks down at you—and a solid, nonexpanding bullet will reach the small brain, dropping the beast in its huge tracks. Visit a museum prior to your hunt to view that brain cavity from different angles.

RIFLES AND CARTRIDGES FOR THE TRICERATOPS

At the very least, a smart hunter of the Triceratops will use a 400-grain bullet, with a sectional density of 0.300, at a minimum muzzle velocity of 2,250 fps. Good choices for the bottom of the scale are the .416 Rigby, .416 Remington, .404 Jeffery, and .425 Westley Richards. Better yet, go with the .458 Winchester Magnum, .458 Lott, or .450 Rigby, delivering a 500-grain bullet at a muzzle velocity between 2,100 fps and 2,400 fps. If a shooter can handle the .500 Jeffery or .505 Gibbs, well, I'll sleep better.

In double rifles, look to the .500-.416 Nitro Express as a minimum, with the .450 NE and .470 NE making a much better choice. The Triceratops is a glaring example of the usefulness of the really big double-rifle cartridges, starting with the .500 Nitro Express up through the .577 Nitro and culminating with the .600 and .700 Nitro Express. Those big guns can be an absolute chore to carry, but when the chips are down, they show their value. Know your recoil limit and use the biggest cartridge—a monometal solid of appropriate

weight—you can shoot effectively to cleanly take a trophy Triceratops. A .600 NE is only as good as the shooter carrying it; place that cartridge in the wrong place and that big gun is absolutely useless.

As a last note, there is a famous image of Hollywood director Steven Spielberg sitting next to a trophy Triceratops. I'm sure everyone's seen it. It's been touted as a movie-set photo, yet I'm here to tell you that it is from an actual hunt. Hollywood characters stumbled across a live Triceratops as they were doing research for *Jurassic Park*. You can take that to the bank.

The author has had very good Triceratops results using North Fork Cup Solids in the .470 Nitro Express.

The Perfect Shot for Dinosaurs

Famous modern dinosaur hunters.

189

Be sure to enter your dino trophy in
*Rowland Ward's Records of Big Game
Dinosaur Edition*

Coming out in 2119

A list of measurers, measuring guides,
and forms can be found at:

rowlandward.com

Rowland Ward
Phone 714-894-9080
info@rowlandward.com

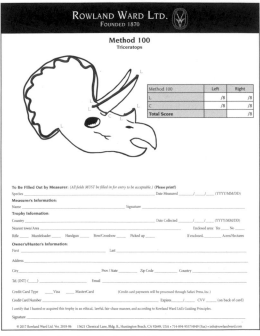

Go to rowlandward.com to download the measurement forms.

ROWLAND WARD LTD.
FOUNDED 1870

Method 101
Parasaurolophus

L

C

Method 101	Left	Right
L	/8	/8
C	/8	/8
Total Score		/8

To Be Filled Out by Measurer: *(All fields MUST be filled in for entry to be acceptable.)* **(Please print!)**

Species _____ Date Measured ____/__/__ (YYYY/MM/DD)

Measurer's Information:

Name _____ Signature _____

Trophy Information:

Country _____ Date Collected ____/__/__ (YYYY/MM/DD)

Nearest town/Area _____ Enclosed area: Yes ___ No ___

Rifle ___ Muzzleloader ___ Handgun ___ Bow/Crossbow ___ Picked up ___   If enclosed, _____ Acres/Hectares

Owner's/Hunter's Information:

First _____ Last _____

Address _____

City _____ Prov / State ___ Zip Code _____ Country _____

Tel. (INT) (___) _____ Email _____

Credit Card Type ___ Visa ___ MasterCard   (Credit card payments will be processed through Safari Press, Inc.)

Credit Card Number _____ Expires ___/___ CVV ___ (on back of card)

I certify that I hunted or acquired this trophy in an ethical, lawful, fair-chase manner, and according to Rowland Ward Ltd.'s Guiding Principles.

Signature _____

© 2017 Rowland Ward Ltd. Ver. 2018-06   13621 Chemical Lane, Bldg. B., Huntington Beach, CA 92649, USA • 714-894-9557/4949 (Fax) • info@rowlandward.com

ROWLAND WARD LTD.
FOUNDED 1870

Method 102
Tyrannosaurus rex

C

L

Method 102	Left	Right
L	/8	/8
C	/8	/8
Total Score		/8

To Be Filled Out by Measurer: *(All fields MUST be filled in for entry to be acceptable.)* **(Please print!)**

Species _____ Date Measured ____/__/__ (YYYY/MM/DD)

Measurer's Information:

Name _____ Signature _____

Trophy Information:

Country _____ Date Collected ____/__/__ (YYYY/MM/DD)

Nearest town/Area _____ Enclosed area: Yes ___ No ___

Rifle ___ Muzzleloader ___ Handgun ___ Bow/Crossbow ___ Picked up ___   If enclosed, _____ Acres/Hectares

Owner's/Hunter's Information:

First _____ Last _____

Address _____

City _____ Prov / State ___ Zip Code _____ Country _____

Tel. (INT) (___) _____ Email _____

Credit Card Type ___ Visa ___ MasterCard   (Credit card payments will be processed through Safari Press, Inc.)

Credit Card Number _____ Expires ___/___ CVV ___ (on back of card)

I certify that I hunted or acquired this trophy in an ethical, lawful, fair-chase manner, and according to Rowland Ward Ltd.'s Guiding Principles.

Signature _____

© 2017 Rowland Ward Ltd. Ver. 2018-06   13621 Chemical Lane, Bldg. B., Huntington Beach, CA 92649, USA • 714-894-9557/4949 (Fax) • info@rowlandward.com

Go to rowlandward.com to download the measurement forms.

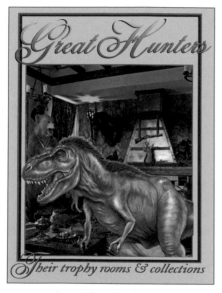